CREATE YOUR OWN
Life Recipe
AFTER DIVORCE

Jasmine Rice

Copyright © 2021 Good Things Are Gonna Come, LLC.

All rights reserved. No part of this book may be reproduced, stored, or transmitted by any means—whether auditory, graphic, mechanical, or electronic—without written permission of both publisher and author, except in the case of brief excerpts used in critical articles and reviews. Unauthorized reproduction of any part of this work is illegal and is punishable by law.

Photography by Aspen Art Co., 2021.

DEDICATION

People come in and out of your life for a reason, a season, or a lifetime. Many people who are no longer a part of my world have made a significant impact on who I am today. This book is dedicated to all of them—everyone who has ever played a role in my life; those who are still a part of my world; and those who now exist only in my memories.

A special dedication goes to Ryan, aka Ray. You have been my biggest supporter from the day *Good Things Are Gonna Come* went from a thought in my brain to a reality. You have always believed in what I have to offer the world and encouraged me to follow my passion. Thank you for being you and for all of the support you give me.

Never forget someone who believes in you when you are a work in progress.

YOUR LIFE RECIPE

SERVING: 1

PREP:
Introduction vii

INGREDIENTS:

1. Loss 1
2. Grief 5
   i. Let's Break Down the Stages 9
3. Relationships 18
   i. Part One: Friends 19
   ii. Part Two: Intimate 25
   iii. Part Three: Yourself 29
4. Health 36
   i. Part One: Diet 37
   ii. Part Two: Exercise 40
   iii. Part Three: Mental Health 45
5. Emotions 48
6. Self-Care & Self-Improvement 54
   i. Part One: Self-Care 55
   ii. Part Two: Self-Improvement 61
7. Journaling 66
8. Comparison 73

9	Impermanence	80
10	Flexibility	87
11	Gratitude	93
12	Choices	99
13	Fast-Forward	105
14	Be Kind	110
15	Quitting	116
16	Boundaries	121
17	Forgiveness	127
18	Head-Heart-Gut	133
19	Mindset	137

COOK:

Tweak Your Recipe	145
Conclusion	149

NUTRITIONAL FACTS:

Encouragement	153
Works Cited	155

INTRODUCTION

*Life is like art. It's never perfect and
it's all about interpretation.*

life
noun
the sequence of physical and mental experiences that make up the existence of an individual.

recipe
noun
a set of instructions for preparing a mixture of ingredients. something which is likely to lead to a particular outcome.

INTRODUCTION

The door opened with a rushed greeting. "Come in," my friend said as she ran in the opposite direction toward the kitchen without ever making eye contact with me. As I walked into her house, I smelled smoke coming from the kitchen, which I suspected was the dinner that I was invited over for. I removed my coat and walked into her kitchen to find her pulling a beautifully burnt lasagna out of the oven and setting it on top of her stove.

I opened her sliding glass door a crack and said, "Mm smells good," in a jesting tone that I sometimes use (though not everyone understands my sense of humor).

My friend slumped down against her cabinets, landed on the floor, and started crying. I quickly sat down next to her and assured her that she was going to be okay. It was just lasagna. To which she responded, "Why can't I do anything right?"

At that moment I realized her sadness was no longer about the lasagna. It was about her recent divorce.

I hugged her without saying any words and just let her cry. After a few minutes of holding her close, I looked at her tear-stained cheeks and said, "When life burns your lasagna, you make something else amazing! You get to create a new recipe!"

I was not just referencing the lasagna she had spent hours making that day (including a sauce from scratch), but I was also referring to life burning her in ways she could never imagine.

I stood up and grabbed her hands. Pulling her up off the ground, I said, "Let's make pasta!"

She smiled. Wiping her tears, she gave a tiny laugh and said, "Let's just order pizza tonight."

Sometimes, your recipe might be a pizza delivery!

There are (give or take) 12,047,578 self-help books out there, and each one of them says something a little different about how to approach grief, self-improvement, self-care, and personal growth. Most books are designed to help you acquire new information. Some are made with the hope of inspiring you. Having the expectation that you are going to find everything you need to "fix" yourself, make you whole again, change your life, or give you all the direction you desire in one book—unfortunately—doesn't exist. Believe me, I have looked!

You won't find one book, podcast, blog, or person out there who can give you all the answers to life and how you should live it. This book, by contrast, is designed to remind you that navigating challenging transitions, self-improvement, self-care, personal growth, or transformation are processes unique to you. You get to create your own life recipe.

When I went through three years of enormous transition, including a divorce and job loss, I looked to self-help books, blogs, podcasts, coaches, therapists, and more to "fix" me. I grew frustrated with the contradictions I found and even threw one book across the room (more on anger in Chapter 2). I had immersed myself in self-help, yet I felt more alone and confused than ever.

It wasn't until months of sorting through my own thoughts—and processing the 484 books I'd read—that I realized no one was going to be able to "repair" me. That was up to me!

Of course, they could all be used as tools to help guide

INTRODUCTION

me, but I needed to find my own recipe—one that worked for me. This book offers my thoughts, experiences, research, and soft suggestions. It's *my* way of navigating this thing we call life after it threw shit my way. I outline pieces of my journey, how I shifted my mindset, and created my own life recipe—something I will forever be tweaking. I wrote this book with the hope of using my experiences to help at least one other person navigate a challenging life transition.

Though I share tips and offer activities to explore, my book is not me telling you what you should do as you navigate these uninvited experiences. Instead, my book gives you a different perspective and tells you that you won't find all your answers in one place. You have limitless opportunities to explore and try lots of different ingredients to create your own life recipe! I'm not promising you anything in this book. I'm not going to say that if you do X for the next thirty days, you will have it all figured out. Or after reading this book, that you will have all the answers. We are all unique and promising something like that is false advertising (in my opinion). Healing takes time. We all have unique needs that develop on our own unique schedules.

What I pledge is that, after reading this you will feel a little better. Maybe not "Let's conquer the world" better, but I honestly believe that you will feel better knowing that when life is hard (*really* hard sometimes), it's okay to take breaks, to step away, to cry, to get angry, to not have the answers, and to know that you aren't alone.

***

I could only hear the "click click click" of my heels as I hurried into my office building. It was eerily quiet at 6:45 a.m. in February, and I usually didn't head into the office this early, but I couldn't sleep. Insomnia was new for me.

I had been crying all morning, and my tear-stained cheeks burned when the cold hit them. I was almost to the building when suddenly, my legs would no longer move. They gave out on me. I collapsed, clutched my chest, and couldn't breathe. At the time, I had thought I was having a stroke or heart attack. Grabbing the fence by the sidewalk to try to lift myself back up, I could feel my chest tighten more. I couldn't speak. White stars flashed all around my vision, and it was as if I had floated out of my body. I felt like I was looking down at myself. I saw my tan coat and red scarf as I clutched my chest. Then someone asked me, "Are you okay?" Like flipping a switch I was back in my body, gasping for air.

That cold February day came two days after separating from my husband. I wasn't having a heart attack. I was having a panic attack. I was scared. I was 95% sure I wasn't going to be able to make it through the divorce. I felt all alone.

Little did I know, in that moment, that I was the one crying on the floor over the burnt lasagna.

I had heard of them before, but panic attacks were new to me. They weren't anything I had ever experienced during my marriage. My wedding day had been one of the happiest days of my life. Even though I'm no longer married that doesn't negate the love and happiness I felt on that day. June 27, 2004 will forever be one of my favorite days.

My (now ex-) husband and I had finally moved to Colorado and were getting married in Breckenridge at a venue overlooking beautiful Lake Dillon. Its mountain backdrop looked like a perfect painting. I met Drew when I was fifteen-years-old. We both grew up in small towns outside of Topeka, Kansas. We began dating when I was seventeen, went to college together at the University of Kansas, moved to Colorado, and got married. Fourteen years later, we divorced.

I loved him and he loved me. But sometimes, life just doesn't work out how you plan.

In my deep-dive through various self-improvement resources I spent most evenings drinking too much wine and reading articles or podcasts on divorce recovery. The reality was that they just pissed me off. I was so angry with these people who seemed to have it all figured out. Yes, they had gone through their own hardships, but they were on the other side of it. I was so angry with them, I wanted to fast-forward through my pain to get to the other side, so I would stop hurting.

On my first solo trip after my separation, I drove in my car to Telluride and listened to a Brené Brown CD I had borrowed from a friend. I was so frustrated with her soothing voice and her uplifting words that I shut the CD off and cranked the radio super loud to prevent me from tossing the CD out the window and yelling, "There is your Rocky Mountain high, Brené!" I was sick and tired of hearing and reading people's happy stories about how everything was going to be okay and how "time heals." I couldn't stand it anymore.

I felt as if these books were contradicting each other: "jump in headfirst and tackle it" vs. "take time for yourself, don't rush." Some of the books even seemed to contradict themselves from one chapter to the next. I was mad that I couldn't talk to someone who was going through, or had gone through, the same situation and didn't yet have it figured out—someone who wouldn't blow smoke up my ass. Who could actually relate to the raw emotions I felt and could say, "This sucks, and it's going to suck for a while. Even though it's so hard to see right now, it's going to get better. It might get worse before it gets better, but you got this!"

[Side note: I really do like Brené Brown, and after I stopped willing her CD to fly out of my window, I was able to gain insight from her books.]

After I got back from Telluride, I decided to give my self-help research another go. I would try to find something inspirational online to listen to and get ready to tackle the week ahead of me in a positive light. That night, I listened to a TED Talk by a woman named Janine Shepherd called *A Broken Body Isn't a Broken Person*. Her inspirational talk details her journey of recovering from a tragic accident to obtaining her private pilot's license—all within eighteen months.

Inspirational, isn't it? Well, at that moment, I said aloud "What the FUCK? Are you kidding me?" I was furious! I cried every day trying to get inspired, and here comes this amazing lady who had her shit together after only eighteen months. NOT FAIR! All I could do in that moment was turn off my computer and cry. I felt so alone, so lost, so defeated. There I was, a divorced forty-year-old woman with no kids.

I spiraled, thinking I was a loser who was going to die alone...

Pity party table of one please! Thanks a lot Janine Shepherd! Now I wanted her and Brené to *both* fly out of my window!

After taking a self-help book hiatus for a few months, I went back and relistened to Janine's talk again because out of all the inspirational books and blogs I had consumed, her eighteen-minute TED Talk stuck with me. After listening to it for a second and then a third time, I started hearing things that made me think, "Maybe I am going to be okay one day."

Now don't get me wrong, I still asked myself, "Why me?" but I was able to absorb more of her story—particularly the part about accepting the circumstances of my life because I couldn't go back and change the past or what had happened to me. Truly, we can't go back and change what has happened to us. It's part of our story now, and all we can do is figure out how to move forward. This journey of healing is hard… some days it sucks. Don't listen to someone who tells you, "You should be over it already," or "Why are you still crying when there are starving children in the world?"

Yes, there are times when I felt guilty for being upset about what I was going through, while there are people in the world who have gone through worse. However, my pain is still real. Your pain is still real. We should all stop comparing our pain to the pain of others. Whatever your grieving process looks like, it belongs to you. There is no chart to tell you when you should feel better.

All that matters is that you are doing something (even something small) each day to heal yourself and move a little further in the right direction. Easier said than done, for sure, but that is why I'm here—to tell you that you aren't alone.

Remember, **You Got This!**

CHAPTER 1

LOSS

Moving forward doesn't mean you forget about losses, life changes, or experiences. It just means that, at your own pace, you accept what has happened and continue living.

> **loss**
> *noun*
> the state of being deprived of or of being without something that one has had.

CHAPTER 1: LOSS

Have you ever had that moment in life when you thought you knew what you wanted, but then a different chain of events happened, and you realized you wanted something else? My ex-husband and I went back and forth on the subject of having children. I wanted them right away in our marriage, and he wanted to wait until he had achieved his career goals.

As the years passed and we both became more successful in our jobs, we traveled more and more, and the discussion about having children came up less and less. I started to accept that our lives had led us in a different direction and kids just might not be on the table for us. That was until I was late one month, peed on a stick, and saw the two lines.

I was very torn in that moment. I was not ready to have a child. Our most recent discussions were about how he worked too many hours; I didn't want to quit my job; I was training for a marathon; and I was getting older. I also had endometriosis and ovarian cysts that could cause some complications, so having a kid wasn't in our plan at that moment.

I instantly became confused and not sure what a baby meant for our life and how it would change. I spent the next few days processing my emotions and talking with Drew about what this would look like moving forward.

A week later I woke up in the middle of the night covered in blood. I knew what was happening. I went to the bathroom and—out of nowhere—started to cry. I was sad that everything was transpiring before I even had time to process all of my feelings. I didn't get a choice in the matter. I had so many emotions, but the one that I was not prepared to feel was loss.

Maybe you've lost your job, a loved one, a marriage, or had a miscarriage of your own. You've lost something in life, even if it was your direction. No one likes experiencing loss. Loss usually takes us by surprise. No one wakes up saying, "I really hope I lose something today!" Recovering from any type of loss takes time, and although recovery might seem like an unattainable goal, our losses make us stronger (even though it's almost impossible to see while we are navigating through them).

Our educational system does not teach us how to deal with loss. No one gives us a *Life 101* book at birth that prepares us for the messy parts. Come to think of it, there isn't a book that prepares us for the good parts either. Nothing teaches us how to overcome life's challenges and losses. We figure it out through experience.

As I struggled through the loss of my divorce, I Googled all the "what to do when" scenarios, and I would get upset when I didn't find the answer I wanted. I was looking for ways to FIX myself quickly. Sort of like people who want a "get rich quick" scenario. That was me.

GOOGLE: Don't blame yourself.
ME: How can I NOT blame myself? Screw that! Look at my life right now. This was not the plan!
GOOGLE: Create value from this experience.
ME: Value? You want me to create value out of something that keeps waking me up at night and causing me to eat potato chips at 2:00 a.m.? Yeah, right!

I found that I was just getting angry. Sure, when you read the lists, they sound great in theory. But I was overwhelmed by the lists because they were suggesting things (that sure, I knew I should be doing) like "realize this too shall pass," which made me want to scream!

"How do they know that? They don't know that!"

So, what do you do when you're in a situation like I was in? You don't want to stay stuck and have loss overtake your life, but how do you move forward? You have to put in the work! I know you are saying, "Put in the work…AHHH!! I don't want to put in the work. I'm exhausted!! I just need to read a book and have it fix me!"

Sorry my friend, that isn't the way it works.

You don't get a six-pack from doing fifty sit-ups. It takes time, consistency, and work to change yourself whether physically, mentally, or emotionally. But the exciting news is you get to create your own recipe! You get to take bits and pieces from all the resources at your disposal to create this beautiful next chapter of your life that will be all your own.

Transforming yourself starts today.

You Got This. Really, you do!

CHAPTER 2

GRIEF

You can be broken and put back together.
You aren't going to look like the original, but why would you want to?

> **grief**
> *noun*
> mental suffering or distress over affliction or loss; sharp sorrow; painful regret.
> a cause or occasion of keen distress or sorrow.

I was eight-years-old when our family dog died. My parents got Cassidy as a puppy before they had children. He was there from the time I was born, and when he was sixteen, he was gone. I remember feeling this loss that I couldn't explain. The hurt inside my chest didn't stop when I got a popsicle or a hug. It was still there.

The first few days after his passing, I would wake up in the morning thinking he was still alive and want to go feed him. When it hit me that his passing wasn't a dream, my heart would ache. I would sit by his grave and cry and talk to him, wishing he would just come back to life.

Of course—he never did.

Eventually the ache became less, but the memories of Cassidy never went away (even to this day).

On average it takes one year for every five to seven years of marriage to get over the loss and finally move on.

Personally, I think that's a load of crap! Sometimes people want to get divorced. It can be 100% a mutual decision where they split on good terms and don't have a lot to grieve, while another couple can face a devastating, unexpected divorce that takes years to move forward from. Who the fuck came up with that formula? Probably someone who's never been divorced.

When I woke up the morning after my husband and I separated, for at least five minutes, I lay there in bed, trying to convince myself it was all a dream like I did with Cassidy. After replaying the previous night's discussion over and over, I was finally lucid enough to accept that it hadn't been a dream. This morning routine of remembering would happen over and over again for the next several months.

To help me get over my divorce, my first go-to was (you guessed it!) to turn to trusty Google and ask, "How to get over a divorce," which (in return) promoted thousands of links with the "Top Tips" on what to do:

1. **Be patient with yourself**
2. **Adjust your expectations**
3. **Accept what you cannot change**
4. **Find strength in others**
5. **Don't get stuck**
6. **Create value from this experience**
7. **Don't blame yourself**
8. **Confront your emotions**
9. **Own your new reality**
10. **Let go of the past**
11. **Eat healthy**
12. **Exercise**
13. **Accept that the pain is normal**
14. **Realize this too shall pass**
15. **Give yourself time to heal**
16. **Forgive**
17. **Let go of the past**
18. **Join a support group**
19. **Pray**

My response that first week to this list was, "How about you shove it up your ass Google?"

CHAPTER 2: GRIEF

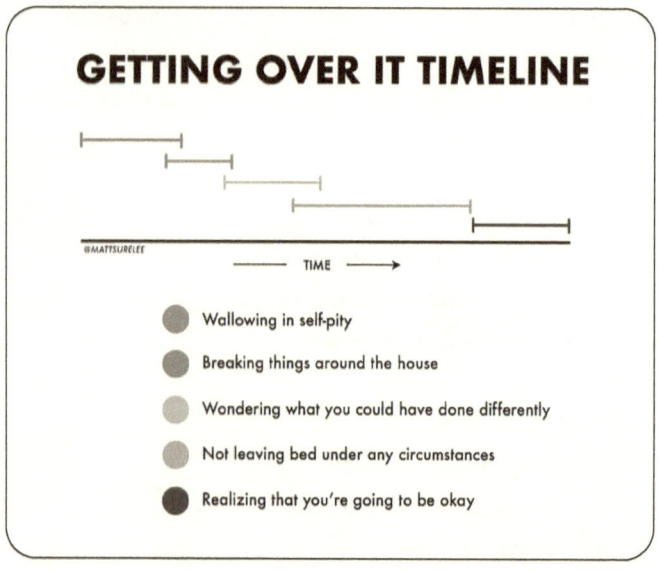

If it were only as easy as this chart, right? In no way am I making light of grief. I have been there. Deep, deep in there. This chart was created with the help of my friend, Matt Shirley, who creates charts about life. He takes real-life situations that can be challenging or overwhelming, and gives them a fun twist in hopes that he makes you smile. Check out his website to see his book! Check out my list of resources in the back for his website.

Mental health specialists talk of the stages of grief, leading you to believe that you are on a steady journey forward, graduating from one stage before you move on to the next. However, the process is not linear. It's more like a rollercoaster taking you up and down. When you're going through the stages of grief, you might believe you've already come to acceptance yet, the next day, find yourself back at the "Not leaving bed under any circumstances" stage.

You don't graduate from one stage and move on to the next. You can go back and forth, you can go out of order, you can even get stuck in one stage for a while. There is a roadmap of sorts, but there are a lot of routes you can choose to take.

Let's Break Down the Stages

Denial
When you're going through the stages of grief, denial helps you survive. In this stage, things don't make sense, you go a little numb, and it's as if what is happening isn't reality. Denial helps you pace your feelings of grief. It's nature's way of letting in only bits and pieces of the hurt, slowly preparing you for the upcoming stages. This is your survival mode keeping you afloat.

Anger
Anger is one emotion we experience from birth, but there is something sort of cute about an angry baby; not so much an angry adult. We're told that, as adults, we need to control our anger, making us a society that fears anger and looks at it in a negative light. But anger is a necessary state in the healing process.

Underneath anger is pain. Feeling anger is a hell of a lot more invigorating than feeling pain. We are often told to suppress anger rather than feel it, but the more you allow yourself to feel it, the more it will dissipate, and the more you will heal.

While obtaining my psychology degree, we were taught that anger is a secondary emotion. A secondary emotion is an emotion that is driven by other feelings. What this means is that, when a person feels angry they are also experiencing other emotions that cause them to feel angry. Anger can be an easier emotion to express because it can energize you, it can ignite you, or it can motivate you.

When Anger Can Be Beneficial

- **Physically**
  Anger helps you cope with stress by releasing tension in your body. Have you ever yelled in your car when no one could hear you or screamed into a pillow? There's a physical release of endorphins when you scream. By screaming, you're calming your nervous system. (I'm not suggesting yelling AT someone; this should be when you're alone.)

- **Motivation**
  Anger serves as a positive motivator. You might be angry that the scale says a certain number and commit to losing weight. Or it can motivate you to remove yourself from an abusive or dangerous situation.

- **Anger Drives You Toward Goals**
  You didn't get what you wanted, and you got pissed? Anger is a trigger that pushes you to try harder. You didn't get the promotion at work, so you work harder or shift direction and get a new job.

To be clear, it's okay and natural to feel and express your anger, but not if it's boiling over in a destructive way where you're lashing out at others. Anger is a completely normal, healthy, human emotion. But not when it turns destructive.

Tips to Keep Anger from Becoming Destructive

- **Breathe**
  If you notice your anger is sticking around just a bit too long, breathe. Yes, you breathe to stay alive, but what I'm suggesting is DEEP BREATHING. Take three deep breaths in through the nose and out through the mouth. If you're in a place where you can close your eyes, even better. The deep breathing allows more carbon dioxide to enter your blood, and stimulate your parasympathetic nervous system.

- **Laugh**
  Redirect your attention to something that will make you laugh. Turn on a comedy skit, reach out to someone in your life who can lighten your mood, or try something like laughter yoga. Denver Laughs is a yoga club that teaches "Laughter Yoga" to help

with stress. There are also a ton of YouTube videos about it, so you can try it out in the comfort of your own home.

- **Exercise**
  Endorphins are our body's natural painkillers that are produced in response to physical discomfort. However, they also play an important role in reducing stress, anxiety, and anger. Even doing something as simple as taking a walk to get your body moving can help.

When you're feeling angry, express it in a non-destructive way, then take the time to reflect and understand why you are angry. Next, be proud of yourself for expressing yourself authentically. Then, choose healthy ways to move out of your anger and keep it from becoming destructive.

If you need help, there's no shame in that! Learning to control anger can be challenging for some, so don't be afraid to seek support if you need it.

The truth is: anger is natural, and you don't need to feel guilty about getting angry from time to time. It's a genuine emotion and you are probably guilty of toxic positivity if you tell the world that you never get angry.

Bargaining

"What if" statements are your way of trying to bargain with God, a higher being, or whatever you believe in, so that they can take you back to the life that you had, so you will stop feeling pain.

We bombard ourselves with "what if" statements. *What if I was a better wife? What if I had left my job a year ago? What if we'd gone to the doctor sooner to find the cancer?*

Guilt creeps in during this stage, and we blame ourselves for failing to do something we think we should have done to prevent the situation we're in.

Depression

After bargaining, empty feelings sneak in, and grief enters your life on a deeper level. Depression feels like it will last forever. This is a stage your support system may struggle with as they wonder when you will "snap out of it."

Though depression is a normal stage, if you find that you're in this stage for too long, and darker thoughts creep in, please talk to someone. Anti-depression medication is not necessary for everyone, but it may help if the depression persists and causes unhealthy thoughts. If you aren't comfortable talking with a friend or don't have the resources to talk to a therapist, please call the National Suicide Prevention Hotline. Their services are free, and they are there for you to talk to them: **1-800-273-8255.**

Acceptance

Acceptance is often confused with the notion of being "alright" with what has happened. This is not the case. Most people don't ever feel "alright" about a loss. This stage is more about accepting the reality that "this" is your new reality, and you can't change the past.

Learning to adjust to your new life is hard, which is why it can take a long time to get to this stage while you are bouncing back and forth between the other stages of grief. At first, finding acceptance may just be about having more good days than bad. Eventually, your life adjusts, and you keep pressing forward with your new reality.

Grieving losses of any kind are difficult and extremely personal. What may cause grief for one person could be taken in stride by another (or at least they handle their grief with minimal stress). We all process differently and at our own pace, and that is OKAY.

Take your time as you move through grief, and allow yourself to feel each of the stages (in whatever order they happen for you), knowing that acceptance doesn't mean you are saying everything is okay. You are simply accepting your new reality. Practicing self-care while grieving can be difficult and overwhelming at times, but try to focus on the basics:

- **Eating:** Healthy foods are great, but during times of grief forgive yourself if you order a pizza—at least you are eating, and comfort food is not always a bad thing.
- **Hydrating:** Water can do wonders. If you are crying you especially need to hydrate. If you aren't a huge fan of water, try putting a little lemon in it or an herbal tea bag to spruce it up.

- **Resting:** Sleep. If you're having trouble with this, there are a lot of natural remedies that can help. A white noise machine can also help calm your mind.
- **Exercising:** I'm not suggesting you go on a five-mile run or do two hours of yoga, which can be overwhelming when you're already struggling with getting out of bed. Try taking a walk around the block to keep your body moving.

Though alone time is necessary and can be healing during grief, don't isolate yourself for too long. Reaching out to supportive friends and loved ones can be extremely beneficial. Give yourself time to sort through these "grief ingredients." Be patient with yourself as you navigate through them. Although you may want to fast-forward to magically being better, going through each stage gives you zest to your knowledge and spice to your strength, so the ingredients for your recipe have more flavor.

If you have a setback or bounce around from stage to stage, it's OKAY. Eventually, you will get to a place of understanding and acceptance that you have lost something significant in your life. Though you can still be sad from time to time when recalling what you have grieved, moving forward is healthy.

Moving forward doesn't mean you forget about your losses, life changes, or experiences. It just means you accept what has happened and continue living. Understanding the stages of grief after loss can be freeing because it gives you a roadmap for understanding your emotions. Take your time as you move through grief. Allow yourself to feel each of the stages knowing that acceptance doesn't mean you are making it okay. You are simply accepting this as your new reality.

These stages are necessary for creating your own life recipe. Avoiding these steps will only prolong your healing process and slow down your transformation. You can bounce around within the different stages as much as you want. No one can tell you how to grieve.

Remember, **You Got This!**

What stage of grief are you currently in?

Have you experienced more than one stage of grief during your current situation? Where have you bounced around the most?

If you have reached the anger stage, how are you expressing it?

What is one thing you could do today that would make you feel better? (Example: take a bath, cry, write a letter to yourself, journal, go on a walk, etc.)

CHAPTER 3

RELATIONSHIPS

I thank you for your part in my journey.

> **relationships**
> *plural noun*
> the way in which two or more concepts, objects, or people are connected, or the state of being connected.

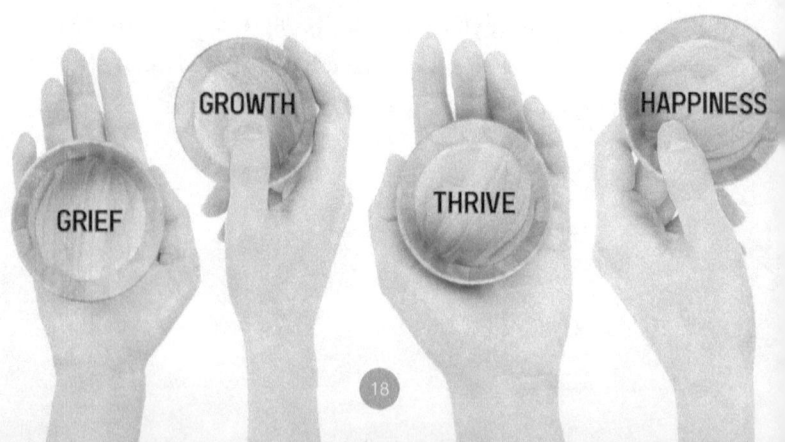

Part One: Friends

Friends come into your life. Some stay, some go.

> Dear Jasmine,
>
> I currently don't have the energy to g   ore to my friendships right now. I fe   friendship has been very one-s   estly, I need more in a fri   focus on myself right now a   into my family and other r
>
> As much as it breaks m   e we acknowledge that our friend hip   for a season versus a lifetime. I'm grateful for the friendship we have had over the last couple of years, and I wish you the peace and love you deserve.
>
> Thank you for everything. I truly wish you all the best.

Asynopsis of a breakup text I received not long after my divorce, when I didn't even realize friends could break up with you. Probably the kindest breakup note someone could receive, nonetheless, still a breakup.

What I can say about the woman who broke up with me is that she was honest and direct. I still respect her immensely, and there are no ill feelings at all. I still think of her fondly, miss her from time to time, and hope that life is treating her with love.

When you are Googling grief, self-care, and personal growth, time and time again you will see the importance of having a solid support network of friends to help you. So, when a friend leaves while you are still navigating challenging times, it's hard.

I have never been one to have a huge network of friends. My parents moved around a lot when I was young. I started school at a one-room schoolhouse with only one other girl in my kindergarten class. How could I **not** be friends with her? She was a bit of a bully to me, but she was my only friend other than my sister, so I accepted it. Because of this, I never really focused on what was important to me in regard to friends. What type of friendships did I want? What was healthy? What was unhealthy? Even with the bullying I experienced, I kept being kind to others. I just wanted people to like me.

After I received the above breakup text, all I could think was: What did I do wrong? What do I do wrong in all my relationships to make people leave me? Mom left when I was a little kid, my husband left, and now my friends were leaving me. I **must** be a shitty person.

I was making it ALL about me!

But when I look back at that note from my friend, I see how kind it was. How honest it was. How hard it probably was for her to write, just as hard as it was for me to read it. I had to respect that she was doing what was best for her.

We think we can smile, be charming, and (*voilà!*) we will have friends. We all want to be liked by everyone. But the truth is, that ain't gonna happen sister!

Some people LOVE friends who are outgoing and spontaneous while others like to have friends who would rather chill over a glass of wine. We all have our preferences on what we want out of our friendships and what they mean to us.

Every self-help book I read told me I needed to have friends—a huge network of them to get me through my divorce, but I don't and that is okay.

I am alright knowing I will never have a huge network of friends. A small close network works for me. Honestly, I'm not sure I have the energy required to juggle a million friendships. I would rather have a few tiers of friends that I'm very close to with whom I can talk to about anything.

- **Virtue friend:** They show **integrity;** someone you're comfortable with and glad to see. They're not someone you would share your most intimate secrets with, but they are close to you.
- **Value friend:** You see them occasionally, you socialize with them, you enjoy and **value** their company.
- **Through friend:** You've known them for a long time, they have helped you **through** times in the past. You don't necessarily connect on a weekly or even monthly basis, but they are there if you reach out. Think of that old high school friend you connected with on Facebook.
- **True friend:** They are in your inner circle; you are your **true** self and share your secrets and struggles with this person.

Take time to look at what types of friends are important to you. Do you have friends who aren't serving you that you need to send a breakup text to like my friend did? It's up to you, but friendships are important in life. Even if you only have a handful of friends.

I know that for me, having a huge network of friends is not a main ingredient in my life recipe. However, I LOVE the friendships I do have. I want to be able to nurture them and give them the energy they deserve. If I had a TON of friends right now in my life, I would feel as if I was spread too thin and not show up in the way I feel friends should. Perhaps that will change as my life changes—remember I get to tweak my own recipe!

I have never broken up with a friend as an adult and, looking back, I can see it might have been beneficial to do so because some of those past friendships were no longer serving me.

The friend breakup was a lesson that taught me that when I invested in myself and learned to love myself and the relationship I had with myself, I would be a better friend, a better daughter, a better partner, and overall a better person for all the relationships in my life.

Letting go of relationships in your life because they aren't serving you is actually very brave. Don't be afraid of losing people, be afraid of losing yourself. You will have different kinds of relationships with numerous people throughout your life. Each one will bring something unique, some good and some bad. Surrounding yourself with a network of people doesn't mean that you need to constantly be talking to or spending time with someone. Having different types of relationships are great: the friend who you can talk to and all they do is nod; the friend who you can sit in silence with and there is such a comfort in the silence nothing needs to be said; and the friend who will give you advice when you ask—each of these people are necessary to your well-being.

When people tell you not to isolate yourself, counter that by saying it's okay to isolate yourself to some extent because alone time is needed when you're processing and navigating challenging transitions in your life. Don't think you HAVE to constantly surround yourself with people, but there is a healthy mix.

Find that balance. If someone is upsetting or draining to you, then maybe you need to step back from that friend. Or maybe you need an alone day to process things by yourself.

Ancient philosophers and scientists agree that one of the keys to happiness is strong relationships with other people. But no one can tell you how many friends you "should" have or what your friendships should look like.

Remember, **You Got This!**

Ingredient Activity

What are 3 important qualities that you want in your "must friends?"

1.

2.

3.

What are 3 important qualities you want in your "just friends?"

1.

2.

3.

Part Two: Intimate

A healthy relationship is with someone who understands your past, shares in your present, and encourages your future.

"How do you like your eggs?"

When I think of relationships, I can't help but think of a scene from *Runaway Bride* with Julia Roberts and Richard Gere. If you haven't seen the movie, the title gives a pretty good idea about the plot. But the egg scene stood out to me because Richard Gere points out that Julia Roberts likes her eggs the exact same way as whomever she is dating. After he points it out, she realizes she doesn't really know how she likes her eggs at all. She doesn't know herself when the movie starts—but she figures it out by the end!

I started dating my ex-husband when I was seventeen. Think back to when you were seventeen. Are you the same person now? I doubt it. We evolve and change as people. Back then (and even until my divorce), I had no clue how I liked my metaphorical eggs.

The Institute for Family Studies found that couples who marry later in life are 50% less likely to get divorced than a couple who marries at the age of twenty. I was married at twenty-five.

Divorce rates within the first ten years of marriage for high school sweethearts were at 54% and were much higher than the average American couple at 32%. Lack of experiences in life and emotional immaturity at a young age can play a part in this. Change is a part of life and either you change and grow together as a couple, or you change and drift apart, no matter what age you are.

If you think after you commit to each other you will just laugh, have a lot of sex, never have any disagreements, and life will be great—you are wrong. Especially on the disagreements part. Relationships of all types take work. If you aren't both willing to put in the work, both of you are going to end up unhappy.

Although it was extremely painful, my divorce taught me so much. That is, once I allowed myself to move forward rather than re-read the last chapters of my life over and over and ask the "what ifs." It made me a stronger version of myself or, as I have said in my blogs, STROFTER. Strong + Soft! (Check out my STROFT blog on my website).

From each of your experiences in life, you learn and grow. You take the happiness, the pain, the smiles, and the tears, and you use them to move on to your next chapter.

So how do you know *what* you want in a romantic relationship?

Well, before you start looking at what qualities are important in someone else, it's more important to know yourself! Know who you are and who you are not. If you are trying to mold yourself and change yourself to fit someone else, it's not going to be a healthy relationship for either of you. You need to figure out what kind of eggs YOU like, and not worry about making someone else's omelet!

When You Get There, What is Important to You in a Partnership?

- **Do you want someone who has a lot of things in common with you, but also has their own interests?**

- **Do you want someone who wants to spend their time with you as well as their friends? Someone who balances their relationships with their alone time?**
- **Do you want someone who pushes you to achieve your goals in a kind and caring way?**
- **Do you want someone who supports you?**
- **Do you want someone who is driven or wants to go with the flow?**
- **Do you want someone who understands a work/life balance or a life/life balance for that matter?**

I think that phrase, "You complete me," is total bullshit, and I've said that since I first saw Jerry McGuire at eighteen. I mean, it *sounds* great, sure. But in the end, you should be a complete person who has a healthy relationship with another complete person. You can certainly complement each other and even feel "whole" when you're together, but you should be complete without someone else.

Keep in mind that a romantic partner can represent multiple things. They can be an asset, an anchor, and even an escape. The more you know yourself before entering into a romantic relationship, the more durable it will be. The longer you are in a romantic relationship, the more likely you will feel settled, which isn't necessarily a bad thing. However, that contentment can quickly lead to stagnation if you fail to be present, communicate, and work on your relationship together.

Cooking up a lasting partnership takes work from *both* sides. A quiche you can bake together!

Remember, **You Got This!**

Ingredient Activity

What are five important qualities you need in a romantic relationship? (Example: affection, appreciation, trust, honesty, humor, consistency, respect, spontaneity, etc.)

1.

2.

3.

4.

5.

Part Three: Yourself

Nourish the relationship with the person that will always have your back. That is the relationship you have with yourself.

At one point in my life (prior to any marriages), my siblings and I all had the same initials: J.J.L. Why my parents thought having four children with the same initials was a good idea is beyond me. My older sister's middle name is Jayne. My younger sister's middle name is Joelle. My brother's is Joseph. And mine is Jude.

I HATED my middle name and always felt so disconnected from it; as if it were a part of myself I didn't know at all. Although we are in an era of self-care, self-love, and embracing who you are, I believe we all have things about ourselves that we struggle to accept or don't quite get. For me, one of those was my middle name—until recently.

"Hey Jude" is a song by The Beatles (in case you've been living under a rock). The song was released in August of 1968 and was number one on the charts for nineteen weeks.

I can't remember the first time I heard "Hey Jude" but I learned pretty early in my life that Paul McCartney wrote it for Julian Lennon, whom he called Jules. He later changed the song from "Hey Jules" to "Hey Jude" because he thought it sounded better. When I found out the song was written for a boy, I hated my middle name even more!

My mom and I were emailing about names not long after my divorce, and she remembered that I didn't particularly care for my middle name. She explained what the song meant to her and why she gave me that middle name. Because the meaning of the song was more important to her than the name "Jude."

Julian Lennon was five-years-old when his parents were going through a divorce, and Paul McCartney wrote this song for him. He encouraged Julian to take his sad situation and try to find comfort, letting Julian know he was going to be okay.

After the email exchange with my mom, I pondered why I felt so disconnected from my middle name. I put so much energy into feeling like I needed to connect with my middle name to know who I was. As if, that would help me "know myself." In reality, it's just a name. But hearing the story about the song made me connect to my middle name more because of the challenge I was facing and overcoming.

I have a different feeling now when I listen to "Hey Jude." It's not that I identify with Julian Lennon, but I have had to view my life the way Paul McCartney encouraged Julian to view his. "Take a bad song and make it better." That has been a part of discovering who I am (and who I am not).

Knowing who you are is not just knowing whether you like chocolate or vanilla, or what type of music you like. It's a journey. It's understanding that you are not the same person you were ten years ago. People change, grow, and evolve. Part of that is knowing not just who you are but, also, who you ARE NOT—which IS a part of knowing who you are.

People often define knowing who they are by identifying what they like. Yes, knowing what brings you joy or pleasure is important, but also knowing what causes you unhappiness or dissatisfaction is just as important. After a difficult life transition, a great way to learn about who you are and who you aren't is to develop a list:

- **I like to live an active lifestyle.**
- **I'm energized by people, but I need an equal amount of down time.**
- **I am a generous person.**
- **I am not a selfish person.**
- **I WILL NOT tolerate someone speaking down to me in a relationship.**

Figuring out who you are in life is a journey, especially when life throws you curve balls. Take a step back and look at how that is going to change your next chapter. The pieces of who you are will join you in your next chapter, and some pieces of who you no longer are will join you as well. A healthy relationship with yourself is valuing yourself as a person and embracing your strengths, while kindly identifying areas where you want to develop and grow.

When I first started dating my ex-husband, I became very co-dependent as I got deeper into the relationship. It reached a point where honestly, I didn't know who I was, and I don't think he knew who he was either. I *thought* I knew who I was. I never felt lost, but looking back my relationship was with him not me.

It wasn't until my divorce that I realized I didn't know who I was. I didn't have a relationship with myself and frankly, I didn't really like myself.

From the time we are young, we want approval from our parents, our friends, and our teachers. Then we grow up and seek approval from our parents, our friends, our bosses, and our partners. What happened to seeking approval from ourselves? Why is it we live life wanting to make other people prouder of us than we want to make ourselves?

How many times in your life have you put your needs or desires to the side to please another person? How many times have you said yes because you were afraid of losing someone or being judged? How many times have you lost yourself to someone or something?

Having a healthy relationship with yourself improves your relationship with others. It's impossible to be 100% emotionally available to others (partners, friends, children) if you aren't connected to and emotionally available to yourself first.

Five Reasons Why the Most Important Relationship is the One You Have with Yourself

1. You're in it for the long haul

Are you ready to have your mind blown? You are the one and only person that will be in your life forever! You literally can never escape yourself. Since that is the case, don't you want the person you spend the most time with to be pretty awesome? Learn to enjoy your own company, learn to enjoy your alone time.

2. I love you, YOU

Self-love and self-care are buzzwords in the personal development community. I am not talking about Narcissus from Greek mythology here. Self-love and self-care aren't narcissistic.

Self-love means **loving yourself unapologetically whereas self-care is about taking the time to feel good in your skin**. While these two are different, they're both necessary. Think of them like making a wedding vow to yourself: "For better or worse, in sickness and in health." You will argue, you will laugh, and in the end, you will be committed to each other forever. It's best to respect, love, and support each other (remember self-love and self-care are about *you*). Because, when shit hits the fan (which it always does at some point), you will be there for you.

3. Hello in there

Only you can hear your thoughts and what are you saying to yourself inside your head. It may feel like enough to have one or one hundred people tell you that you are attractive, smart, and funny. But, until you truly feel like those things inside, you will never believe it. Short and sweet!

4. It does a body good

There are three parts to this, and I'm going to get real.

First, let's talk about diet. You're the only person who knows how bloated you feel after eating a plate of fried food topped off with extra bacon. I'm not suggesting that you should only eat kale and quinoa for the rest of your life, but listen to your body. You'll know what to expect if you do indulge in the loaded cheese fries with sour cream and jalapeños.

Second, let's discuss exercise. I'm a runner, but I'm not telling you to run. Does running hurt your knees? Then listen to your body and don't run! However, you should find some way to move because being physically active makes you feel better. Try new things, experiment, find what you like, and what works for you. But move your body every day.

Third, let's talk about sex—with yourself. If masturbation talk makes you uncomfortable, move on to the next chapter! How are you going to tell someone else what you like, if you don't know what you like yourself? It's a way for you to get to know your body. Not only does it feel amazing, but masturbation can also reduce stress. Orgasms release oxytocin and dopamine. Win, win!

Relationships with family, friends, and a romantic partner can add to your overall happiness in life. But there is one important relationship that is the key ingredient and matters more than any other relationship—that my friend, is the beautiful relationship you have with yourself. By working on this relationship consistently, it's going to enhance all of your other relationships and experiences.

Remember, **You Got This!**

Ingredient Activity

What are the top three non-physical things you love about yourself?

1.

2.

3.

What are the top three physical things you love about yourself?

1.

2.

3.

CHAPTER 4

HEALTH

A healthy outside starts on the inside.
Be kind to your body, it will thank you.

health
noun
the state of being free from illness or injury; a person's mental or physical condition.

Part One: Diet

I was seven-years-old, sitting in a closet hiding from my sister, eating a bowl of butter with sugar on it. I had the closet door cracked but accidently pulled it closed when I heard footsteps. I sat in the dark and ate when I realized my stomach didn't feel great. I tried to leave the closet but was locked in. I freaked out, crying and banging on the closet door until my mom found me.

She stared at the half-eaten sugar/butter mixture and asked why I was in the closet. I explained I wanted something sweet. She helped me out of the closet, and we had a long talk about how bad eating a bowl of sugar and butter was for me.

I have used food as a way to soothe myself my entire life. If I was sad, I would eat! If I was mad, I would eat! If I was stressed, I would eat!

At thirteen I began to binge and purge. I continued this for a couple of years until I learned that it could have permanent effects on your throat (since my dream at that time was to be a singer, I stopped).

I've always had a curvy, athletic build, and (to this day) I'm convinced my bones are made of lead. When I was in college, I worked out twice a day. I ate like a bird. I got down to a size four, was 132 pounds at five-foot-two-inches, and the CDC *still* considered me to be overweight. Throughout high school and college, I tried every diet possible. My freshman year, I only drank SlimFast to ensure I wouldn't gain the dreaded "Freshman Fifteen."

I have yo-yoed with my weight my entire life, always

having a negative view of my body. When my separation happened, I wasn't able to eat for about two weeks, but then, food became my comfort once again. And wine—too much wine!

After putting on a lot of weight in a short amount of time, drinking to the point where I passed out in the bathtub, and losing my hair due to stress and diet, I knew this was not the life I wanted to be living. I needed to change.

I KNEW I would feel better when I went back to eating better and drinking less.

I'm not saying don't eat the donut. Yes, pizza is fucking amazing, and you can still eat it! But I'm suggesting moderation. Give yourself grace when you're going through a challenging time. Food can be comforting, but try your best to balance it with a little healthy food. If you usually eat two donuts, try substituting an apple for one of the donuts.

Feeling better physically also helps you feel better mentally. I indulge in French fries or pizza from time to time, but I know that when I eat clean 75% of the time, I'm going to feel better. Like everything in life, it's about balance. Oh, and drink water, lots of water. It's basically liquid gold and it's free!

Remember, **You Got This!**

Ingredient Activity

What is an example of your current diet?

Breakfast _____

Lunch _____

Dinner _____

Ounces of water a day _____

Number of alcoholic
beverages a week _____

Are you happy with this? If there is one small, healthy change you could make this week (without feeling overwhelmed) what would it be?

Part Two: Exercise

Exercise changes your body.
But even more, it changes your mind.

I have always exercised, but I picked up running when I was twenty-nine after an abdominal surgery left me bedridden for almost six weeks. During my recovery, I watched a documentary on marathons. When my ex-husband got home that evening, I told him I was going to run a marathon, to which he said, "Um, you aren't a runner."

That Christmas, he purchased me a pair of running shoes, a beginner's guide to running a marathon, and a running outfit. Then my training began. I ran my first half-marathon six months later and, a year after that, I completed my first marathon at the age of thirty.

I love being physically active. I have a love/hate relationship with running but honestly, I love it more than I hate it. I also love hiking, yoga, weight training and getting my body moving.

Endorphins are chemicals that act like medically engineered opioids. Endorphin production is one of the ways that our bodies respond to physical discomfort, such as a long run. Runners credit endorphins for their feel-good effects. Some even describe a "runner's high" as an intense, blissful emotional experience similar to an orgasm (I wouldn't go that far, but hey—let's see what happens on my next long run!).

Endorphins are our body's natural painkillers produced in response to physical discomfort. However, they also play an important role in reducing stress and anxiety—both of which you have more of when you are going through a challenging transition. We are constantly bombarded by advertisements for ways to get in shape and stay healthy (both physically and mentally). Yet, according to the Department of Health, only 19% of women and 26% of men currently meet the CDC's physical activity guidelines, which recommend adults get at least 150 minutes of moderate aerobic activity a week.

When you're facing a challenge in your life, exercising might not always be an ingredient you're ready to add to your life recipe (even though you know physical activity is one of the most powerful forces for good health). Physical activity affects our bodies in so many ways. Scientists have found that regular participation in aerobic exercise has been shown to decrease levels of tension, anxiety, and stress; improve sleep; and give you more energy.

A Few Mental Benefits of Exercise:

1. Reduce Stress

Increasing your heart rate can reverse stress by stimulating healthy levels of norepinephrine. Exercise forces the body's central and sympathetic nervous systems to communicate with one another, improving the body's overall ability to respond to stress.

2. Sleep Better

Physical activity helps regulate our circadian rhythm, which controls when we feel tired and alert.

3. Alleviate Anxiety

Here are those endorphins! Exercise has been shown to have more success with reducing anxiety than a bubble bath (and I love my bubble baths!).

4. More Energy

When we exercise, our blood flow increases, which carries oxygen to our muscles and makes us more alert.

There are a lot of little things you can do that don't take a ton of time to keep your body moving. Sixty minutes is great, but thirty minutes is better than fifteen minutes, and fifteen minutes is better than zero minutes. So, let's get moving!

A Few Fun Ideas

- Do sixty seconds of jumping jacks when you get out of bed in the morning.
- Go on a walk around the block, but every two minutes, skip for a bit.
- Do FaceTime pushups: Pick a friend who will bust them out with you before you hang up.
- Have a baby? Do some squats holding them (safely). No baby? Grab whatever you have.
- You're supposed to brush your teeth twice a day for two minutes. Hold a squat that whole time!
- Cleaning the house today? Walk with high knees while you're moving around the house (by the way,

cleaning the house burns about 200 calories an hour *sans* high knees).
- **Really into streaming a new TV series? Do a thirty- to sixty-second plank every time you have to hit pause to refresh your glass of water or go pee!**

Moving my body and eating well (most of the time) makes me feel clearer. I sleep better; it helps me when I'm stressed or overwhelmed; and I have more energy.

But that's ME! Remember this is *your* recipe. It can be daunting to think that after you read this book you are going to put it down, put on your running shoes, knock out a 5k, and drink a protein smoothie. If you already eat healthy, have an active lifestyle, and avoid nicotine but still feel like you are in a rut—change it up! But if you're someone who gets nauseated even thinking about physical exercise, or have other physical limitations you need to focus on, start with something simple like stretching.

Take baby steps.

Remember, **You Got This!**

Ingredient Activity

What is your current exercise routine?

If you are currently exercising on a weekly basis, but are feeling blah about it, what is something you could do to change up your routine?

If you are not currently exercising, what is one thing you could do this week to get your body moving?

Part Three: Mental Health

Take care of your mind, and your body will thank you.

Devotion to your mental health is the best thing you can do for yourself and your body. Mental or emotional health refers to your overall psychological well-being. It can consist of how you value yourself, the quality of your relationships, and your ability to cope with your feelings and deal with this challenging transition in your life. Nurturing your mental or emotional health should be one of your top priorities.

Being mentally or emotionally healthy means more than being free of depression or anxiety. Mentally healthy people often:

- Enjoy life more.
- Have the desire to laugh and seek out fun.
- Are able to work through stressful situations and bounce back from adversity quicker.
- Feel a sense of purpose, in both their relationships and self.
- Are flexible and adaptable to change.

In life, we will all experience disappointment, loss, and unexpected change. These challenges can cause depression, sadness, anger, anxiety, and stress and affect your physical health.

Depression has been found to be associated with an increase of coronary heart disease, and people with higher levels of emotional stress are 32% more likely to die from cancer.

Simple Mental Health Tips

- **Practice self-care.**
- **Disconnect from technology when you can.**
- **Engage in activities that provide meaning to you.**
- **Get help from a licensed mental health professional if you need it. Seeking help is not a sign of weakness. Just as you might seek a personal trainer to help get your body into physical shape, seeking a mental health professional to help get your mind into shape can be equally beneficial.**

Physically healthy people are better able to recover from illness or injury. Similarly, people with strong mental and emotional health are more resilient and can more easily bounce back from adversity, trauma, and stress.

Remember, **You Got This!**

Ingredient Activity

We tend to get overwhelmed when we go through challenging transitions in life because we add things to our plates to help us feel better such as exercise, schedule outings with our friends, therapy, etc. We ADD to our list of things to improve our mental health but, sometimes, all these additions can also add to our stress, making it counterproductive.

List three things you can eliminate from your life this month that will improve your mental health.

1.

2.

3.

CHAPTER 5

EMOTIONS

---

*All emotions play a part
in a fulfilled life.*

> **emotions**
> *plural noun*
> a natural instinctive state of mind deriving from one's circumstances, mood, or relationships with others.

Two years ago, when someone said to me, "This too shall pass," I glared at the patronizing smirk on their face and wanted to smack it off. I'm not a violent person but their words frustrated me. It sounded to me like they were saying, "Come on, Jasmine. Put on your big girl pants. It's just a divorce." They didn't know the specifics of what I was going through! I didn't need their positivity thrown at me like I was a three-year-old throwing a tantrum.

At that moment I was upset, sad, frustrated, and wanted to cry. And that is exactly what I did. I was in no mood to be positive, and I didn't need someone telling me otherwise.

Did you know there is actually a phrase for being TOO positive? It's called **toxic positivity.** Dr. Jamie Long defines toxic positivity as:

> *Excessive and ineffective overgeneralization of a happy optimist state across all situations. The process of toxic positivity results in the denial, minimization, and invalidation of the authentic human emotional experience.*

In layman's terms, if you're having a bad day and don't want to start the day with a positive affirmation or writing down ten things you are grateful for—that is 100% okay! The idea that we should only focus on positive emotions and the positive aspects of our lives is not being authentic.

CHAPTER 5: EMOTIONS

This world needs more kindness, and being positive has been a huge part of my growth journey over the past few years. However, in no way do I think that we are all meant to be happy and smiley every moment of our lives. I encourage my clients to hang on during the bumpy rides, get back up, and keep moving forward the best they can—even when it's hard. But it's also okay to have those days when you need to process everything that's going on in your life without plastering on a fake smile. In other words, sit with your shit!

Toxic positivity went into overdrive in 2020 when COVID-19 reared its ugly head. We were all affected in challenging ways with job loss, loss of loved ones, loss of a physical connection with others, and loss of an emotional connection, too. To keep things positive, we would often hear, "This too shall pass."

However, not acknowledging that you might have been scared, upset, frustrated, hurt, or disappointed when the holidays rolled around in 2020 (and you couldn't see your family) meant you weren't being honest with yourself. There is nothing wrong with counting your blessings during dark times. But you can do that while also acknowledging your discomfort.

This doesn't just go for COVID-19. It goes for all external pressures and internal pressures you're undergoing in *your* personal world. Feel it, express it—but be mindful to not let it consume you long term. Practicing gratitude for what you *do* have is healthy. But also, being authentic and expressing what is troubling you (like missed celebrations or worries about the future in the face of a global pandemic) are equally as healthy.

Be kind to yourself by being honest with your feelings—all of them. Remember how your diet is about balance? Same goes for your emotions. If we are irritated, most of us respond to the question, "How are you doing?" with a flippant, "I'm okay." We don't find it necessary to open up to the grocery store clerk or a co-worker by answering, "Actually, I'm having a pretty shitty day." It's easier to be polite and respond with, "I'm okay."

But here is some food for thought: maybe your answer of "I'm okay," is the truth!

"It's okay to NOT be okay" has become a popular tag line on social media. But I question: doesn't that insinuate that okay equals happy, and any other emotion means not okay (which is bad)?

Maybe "okay" is actually like responding with a passive-aggressive middle finger.

When you are dealing with a divorce, job loss, the effects of COVID-19, or any difficult transition in life, it's perfectly acceptable and necessary to be pissed off, cry, and feel all of your emotions.

But why are those emotions construed as "not okay?"

Stating that "it's okay to NOT be okay" insinuates that feeling grief is not an "okay" emotion to feel. All of these emotions, all of these feelings are not only "okay," they are necessary emotions for healing. Perhaps, the next time someone says to you, "It's okay to NOT be okay," don't be afraid to respond with, "Oh, I'm okay, I might be crying… but that, my friend, *is* okay!"

CHAPTER 5: EMOTIONS

It's perfectly normal and healthy to feel all of your feelings. Yell when you must, get upset when you need to, cry if it helps. If you put on a happy face when you are struggling and sweep your emotions under the rug (even through tragedy), they will eventually boil over.

Remember, **You Got This!**

Ingredient Activity

It's not always possible to express our emotions as they come to us. For example, when you are in a meeting at work and something triggers you, what do you do?

Perhaps you excuse yourself to go to the bathroom, but then you allow yourself to revisit whatever triggered you later tonight when you get home. Give yourself permission to cry or do whatever you need to process that thought in the comfort of a safe space.

Blocking out time to feel or express your emotions gives you power over them rather than allowing them to have power over you.

If you were to schedule a time to allow yourself to feel your feels, what would be the best time for you?

How long would you give yourself?

What would you do during that time?

CHAPTER 6

SELF-CARE & SELF-IMPROVEMENT

Invest in yourself to give the best version of you, not what is left of you.

> **self-care**
> *noun*
> the practice of taking an active role in protecting one's own well-being and happiness; in particular, during periods of stress.

Part One: Self-Care

One night after work in the middle of my divorce, I pulled into the driveway mentally exhausted. I'd had an extremely stressful, challenging day on top of the commute home from hell. All the while, my head was spinning because I was still coming to terms with the fact that I was getting a divorce.

I knew what I had to do when I walked inside: feed the dogs, pack for my upcoming business trip, compose a work email that I needed to send before the morning, and then sort through some of the things in this home I would no longer live in.

As I sat in the garage in my car, I closed my eyes and took a few deep breaths. I cranked up the radio, let a few tears fall, and sat. Sometimes, something as simple as sitting in your car can be self-care.

Prior to the 20th century, self-care within society was linked to affluence and privilege. In some cases, standards such as hygiene, diet, clothing, and education were forced on others through Western society's colonialization of various native countries.

In the early 20th century, self-care was used predominately by physicians on patients who were mentally or chronically ill. The notion was that teaching these patients to foster healthy habits would offer a sense of autonomy over their heavily regulated lives.

In the 1980s, Tony Robbins marketed himself as a peak performance coach and motivational speaker, offering presentations with "self-help" and "positive thinking." As a society we began to measure our "self-care" with terms like: productivity, efficiency, and work-life balance. In the 1990s, we were introduced to *Chicken Soup for the Soul*. If you aren't familiar with this series of books, they offer inspirational, true stories of everyday people's lives. The power those stories have on changing others' perspectives on certain topics is remarkable.

In the last five years, the term "self-care" has been seen on social media, websites, magazines, podcasts, and blogs. There are many different approaches to developing guides and providing tips on the best ways to practice it. These sources tell us it's okay to take time and care for yourself before caring for the rest of the world.

They share self-care tips such as:

- **Get enough sleep each night**
- **Exercise daily or do yoga**
- **Meditate**
- **Eat a healthy diet**
- **Saying no is okay**
- **Get outside more**
- **Get more organized at home and at work**
- **Unplug from social media**
- **The list goes on....**

These viewpoints tell us that taking the time to take care for ourselves is vital—especially if we want to take care of anyone or anything else. However, what is missing from these narratives is information about including others in your self-care practices. Some people get anxious when they try to follow a "Top 10 List" of things that are traditionally seen as self-care because they aren't stress-relieving for them.

So, what is the self-care concept that has been around for so long, yet has only been a trending hashtag recently?

Self-care is not something you can just go purchase at a store. It includes a variety of activities tailored for each individual. True self-care is figuring out what resonates with you. Honor what *your* needs are and work on those needs within your *boundaries*.

Also, there is nothing that says self-care must be done all alone. Sure, self-care is all about your*self*, but friends can be a huge part of your self-care strategy.

Self-care is often viewed as alone time, but relationships play an important part in our mental health.

If being around friends causes your stress level to decrease, and you feel re-energized and relaxed around them, then why not call your friend to get an outing on the schedule?

Just as you get to create your own recipe for a fulfilling, happy life that you don't want to escape from, you also get to slice and dice your own recipe for self-care.

There are a million different books, blogs, and podcasts on how to practice self-care. They are tools that offer suggestions and allow you to pick and choose what works for you.

- **If massages make you anxious, don't get them.**
- **If you're allergic to every tree in nature and hiking makes you break out in hives, don't hike.**
- **If you start a gratitude journal and realize you keep making a grocery list, then put the pen down.**

- **If you tried meditating and, every time you say "Om," you immediately hear Cookie Monster saying, "Om nom nom nom nom," maybe skip the meditation.**
- **If sitting in your car can help you reset, then by all means sit.**

Find things that work for you. If you search the internet for tips and, after trying them, you are more anxious, stop doing them.

Self-care is not about self-improvement. It's not about "fixing" yourself. It's more about taking care of yourself in whatever way feels right to you. Do things that evoke a sense of peace inside of you—things that "reset" you and help you to feel more joyful about your life as a whole.

I'm not going to provide you with the "Top 10 Ways to Practice Self-Care" because my list would be *my* self-care recipe, which wouldn't necessarily benefit you. You get to create your own delicious gourmet pizza with your own personal toppings.

Self-care is how you fuel your self-love, so you are able to share your love with everyone around you. Your heart is warm when you are able to show up with generosity, patience, and compassion for the ones you love. But you must remember that it's impossible to truly be there for others without taking care of yourself first.

- **You take care of yourself by asking what your needs are.**
- **You take care of yourself by making healthy choices for your body and mind.**

- **You take care of yourself by lightening up and not being so damn hard on yourself.**

At times, life can feel overwhelming or seem like a never-ending to-do list. How do you find the time to fit in self-care? You learn to disrupt the downpour of life's demands in order to replenish yourself, so you can fully show up for all of your passions and responsibilities.

You can't be the best you when you live your life running on fumes. If you need your pot of water to boil, you wouldn't turn on the gas stove without lighting it, would you?

Self-care is a necessary action of self-love. Your water needs to boil; therefore, it requires that match.

Ingredient Activity

What are five things you do to practice self-care? Remember, these can be as simple as showering or brushing your teeth every day.

1.
2.
3.
4.
5.

Now, what are five things you COULD be doing to practice self-care right now. Be realistic here. Don't write down things you aren't willing to commit to.

1.
2.
3.
4.
5.

Part Two: Self-Improvement

Let's not get self-care confused with self-improvement. I've spent hundreds of dollars on self-help books, seminars, and retreats over the past three years. I've devoted thousands of hours to reading blogs and listening to podcasts about personal growth and self-improvement all with the goal of finding the answers that would "fix" me.

After my divorce, I became addicted to the idea that the answer to my happiness and healing was in a book, podcast, or blog. I kept waiting to read or hear that magic "ah-ha!" tip that would change my life forever.

Hi, I'm Jasmine. And I'm a recovering self-improvement addict.

When I faced several unexpected challenging transitions in my life (all in a very short period of time), I became compulsively consumed with self-improvement and personal growth.

Don't get me wrong, some of the most powerful breakthroughs I've had in my personal growth have been due to a seminar I attended, a book I read, or a life coach that I worked with. But it was as if I was never satisfied with what I read or heard. I wanted MORE, MORE, MORE!

Self-improvement is wanting to improve upon your knowledge, thought patterns, or character through your own efforts. The goal is to reach a point where you no longer feel the need to improve yourself, comparable to nirvana. A transcendent state in which there is no longer desire. It's as if some people strive to get a "Self-Improvement PhD" and believe that their life will be perfect once they have one.

CHAPTER 6: SELF-CARE & SELF-IMPROVEMENT

If you find that you are picking yourself apart and comparing yourself to others when you are reading self-help books, is that really helping? Can self-improvement poison your mind?

Merriam-Webster's Dictionary defines addiction as "a compulsive, chronic, physiological or psychological need for a habit-forming substance, behavior, or activity having harmful physical, psychological, or social effects and typically causing well-defined symptoms (such as anxiety, irritability, tremors, or nausea) upon withdrawal or abstinence: the state of being addicted."

When you think of an addict, you probably envision someone who is addicted to alcohol, drugs, or sex. Not a forty-something professional who reads *Girl, Wash Your Face* before turning in for the night. Placing importance on self-improvement doesn't necessarily mean that you're addicted. When looking at whether or not you are addicted, ask yourself: do you keep repeating the same patterns and behaviors no matter how much you try to develop yourself?

According to Market Research, the self-improvement market in the United States was worth $9.9 billion in 2016 with an estimated growth projection of $13.2 billion by 2022.

If it works so well, why are people constantly waiting for the next self-help best seller by Tony Robbins to be released or the next TED Talk by Brené Brown to go live? Wouldn't you only need to read one book or listen to one seminar to achieve self-improvement nirvana? The truth is that self-improvement, personal growth, and self-care are all constantly changing. That's why there are millions of book options and thousands of seminars with different approaches.

It's healthy to want to continue developing yourself, but do you ever take time to be in the present and appreciate who you are in that moment? Take a minute to process the tips and tools you have read and reflect on how you want to implement them into your life before you buy the next best seller.

I'm certainly not suggesting you should never purchase another self-help book again, but keep in mind, those books, blogs, podcasts, and seminars can only give you ideas, suggestions, and recommendations. YOU'RE the one who has to put all of it into motion. Those tools are someone else's opinion on what you *should* do, or what *could* work for some people. They are just that—opinions.

If you have focused on self-improvement for quite some time and feel as if it may be taking over your life, I encourage you to take a break. In your efforts to continually improve, you can end up sending yourself the message that you are not enough, you are lacking, or you are not worthy just as you are. As you take time to slow down and look at all that you are trying to improve, it can be helpful to allow yourself to look at the ways you are succeeding in life and give yourself credit for even the baby steps you've taken so far.

Solely placing importance on self-improvement doesn't mean you have an addiction. Accepting yourself doesn't mean that you stop growing or improving. Self-acceptance simply means that you're able to look at the big picture and acknowledge your strengths in conjunction with the areas you would like to develop. Acceptance doesn't mean that you

CHAPTER 6: SELF-CARE & SELF-IMPROVEMENT

can't still read the books, listen to podcasts, and attend seminars to develop who you are. It means that you allow yourself to also see the amazing qualities you currently have today. Striving to develop yourself and work on self-improvement can be positive if you are balancing it with acceptance. It becomes toxic when it becomes your addiction.

Self-improvement can become a never-ending project; you can always find something else that needs to be changed. To break the self-improvement addiction, you have to take a step back and decide to be happy with who you are now.

Remember, **You Got This!**

Ingredient Activity

What is something that you can 100% accept about yourself right now?

CHAPTER 7

JOURNALING

Journaling is the combination of speaking and listening at the same time.

> **journaling**
> *noun*
> a daily record of news and events of a personal nature; a diary.

I received my first journal when I was thirteen-years-old. It was pink and white with a Velcro clasp on it—as if that would keep my younger sister out; she really wanted to read the juicy details of the boy I had a crush on. I wrote in that journal religiously for about a month. Daily turned into weekly, which turned into monthly. As more time passed, my pretty pink and white journal began to collect dust.

Fast forward twenty-five years: I'm experiencing a major life transition, and just about every self-help book I read suggests that for personal growth, self-discovery, and overcoming grief, journaling is the way to go.

I was given a small journaling book from a friend for my fortieth birthday. The idea was to write one sentence each day about how I was feeling or something that stood out about my day. I wrote in it every day for about a month, and then the same thing happened to my *One Line A Day* journal that happened when I was thirteen. My daily entries turned into weekly entries, which turned into monthly entries. The last entry I wrote, only two months after receiving the journal was, "I cried today."

I continued to read self-help books, blogs, and listen to podcasts that insisted the key to growth and overcoming struggles in life was journaling. Eventually, I decided to give it another try and purchased a blank journal that said, "You Got This" on the cover.

You probably guessed it—the cycle happened again. I started off strong and as weeks passed, the new journal sat on my bedside table unopened.

When I look back, the struggle I had was that I never understood what I was supposed to write about. I would open my journal and feel overwhelmed by my emotions. I would get anxious whenever I got the pen out and stared at the blank paper.

Then something happened that changed my view on journaling.

One morning after a rough night, I was listening to the radio on the way to work when an ad came on (for some product I can no longer recall), and a woman with a soothing voice said, "If you get tired, learn to rest…not quit."

The quote spoke to me at that moment, and I felt it was timely with everything that was going on in my world. With a foggy head, I didn't want to forget the quote, so I pulled out my phone to record what I had just heard in my voice memos.

As I hit record, I explained what I was doing, recited the quote, and then kept talking into my phone for another two to three minutes. I talked about the rough night I had, how the quote made me feel, and that I was going to be optimistic about the day I was getting ready to face.

When I got home, I pulled out my phone to listen to the quote I had heard, and I realized that I had journaled in audio form. It was a little strange to hear my voice at first, but I really liked hearing the words that flowed out of me so naturally.

The next day, I decided to do it again. I recorded myself for about three minutes talking about the day ahead of me. I didn't have a plan about what I wanted to say, I simply wanted to capture my emotions, feelings, activities, and thoughts. I found a way to journal that worked for me. Instead of forcing myself to open up a physical book and write a sentence about how I was feeling, I hit record and let the words flow out of my mouth.

Journaling can be very daunting to some while others love it. Research studies are mixed on the benefits of journaling, and whether or not you want to try it is completely up to you. Some feel that capturing your thoughts, feelings, and experiences helps you grow. Others believe it makes issues worse if you only journal when you are overwhelmed by only capturing negativity.

Positive Effects of Journaling (Written or Audio)

- **Allows you to evaluate your thoughts, emotions, and behavior**
- **Explores resolutions**
- **Converts negative energy into positive growth**
- **Helps decrease your emotional reactivity to others**
- **Increases acceptance of unpredictability, which is a part of life**
- **Helps you see other people's perspectives**
- **Captures alternative courses of action**

Negative Effects of Journaling (Audio or Written)

- **Makes you live in your head**
- **Renders you a passive spectator of your life**

- **Becomes a vehicle to blame instead of searching for solutions**
- **Causes you to wallow in negative things that have happened to you**

Will journaling work for you? That is for you to decide. If you want to give it a try, maybe don't start with something profound like jotting down your life goals. Instead, start by journaling about your reaction to a family of geese that you saw walking across a busy street. Rather than snapping a photo of it and posting it on Instagram, journal about the smile that was on your face when you watched them all waddle by.

There are No Rules to Journaling

- **Start small**
  If you want to write, start with a sentence or a word. If you want to talk, maybe say one or two words with the date and leave it at that.

- **Make it your own!**
  Let go and write or talk about whatever. If you want to make a gratitude list, great. If you need to vent about something that has been eating at you all day, great. If you want to journal about the weather, that's great, too. Sometimes simply recording your emotions or thoughts can be restorative.

- **Stop if it isn't working**
 Journaling is not for everyone, and that's okay. If you've never tried it and feel stuck, journaling could be worth a shot. And if you don't want to crack open a book and grab a pen, there are some amazing apps out there. If you want, try audio journaling or record in your voice memos like I do.

Why not try capturing your emotions, feelings, actions, frustrations, concerns, and hopes?

Having a schedule can help you create a routine so you are consistent, but again, there are no rules. If you feel setting a time each day is too constricting, go with what works for you. I still have my audio journal and, although I don't record in it daily anymore, I still record weekly and go back to listen to previous entries to see how much I have grown.

Journaling can be a huge part of self-care for some. For me it works, but for others it doesn't. If you are adamant that journaling is not for you, that's okay. But it never hurts to try something new. What do you have to lose?

Remember, **You Got This!**

Ingredient Activity

If you don't currently journal AT ALL, I encourage you, for one week, to spend five minutes either writing or recording your thoughts.

If you currently journal and love it, YAY! You found something that works for you! Keep it up!

CHAPTER 8
COMPARISON

*Stop comparing your journey to others,
you have your own race to run.*

> **comparison**
> *noun*
> a consideration or estimate of the similarities or dissimilarities between two things or people.

CHAPTER 8: COMPARISON

We've all seen her. That mom who runs five miles at 4:30 A.M. and then cooks a three-course meal for breakfast before dropping her kids off at school looking like a runway model. Meanwhile, you're happy that you got to brush your teeth before putting on your yoga pants and pulling your hair into a ponytail while the kids scurry out the door.

I don't have children, but I've talked to my younger sister many times in the morning after her kids have gone to school. She's even sent me a selfie or two of her mismatched outfit and messy hair when she didn't give a shit because she is amazing like that! Nevertheless, in addition to being an amazing mom, my sis is gorgeous all dolled up or in a tank top chopping wood.

In today's society, it's difficult NOT to compare yourself or what you are going through to others. People's "perfect" lives are plastered on TV, social media, magazines, and even seen in person. (Remember, we only see the highlight reels.)

In addition to the "perfect" people we compare ourselves to, we also compare our struggles in life. Dismissing the importance of our own battles or frustrations because we believe someone else's hardship to be more significant. Then we are left feeling guilty for expressing our grief or disappointment as if we aren't worthy of expressing our emotions.

For me, that shifted when I accepted that there is a difference between comparison and perspective.

Comparing your life, your struggles, your journey, or whatever you are experiencing isn't healthy because you diminish what you're going through. However, having a little perspective and being grateful for what you do have or what "good" is happening in your life can assist you when overcoming your difficult situation.

We all experience pain, sadness, grief, and hurt. But why do we feel it's necessary to compare our struggles? I'm not sure anyone wants to place first in *most struggles of the week* and, as a runner, I sure do love me a medal!

I have felt guilty throughout my life for being sad, upset, or hurt about whatever is going on in my life when I know others have it worse. "There are starving children in the world, so stop complaining about your problems!"

I met a recently divorced woman in my apartment complex about one month after my separation. We were discussing our stories, and I was sobbing over what I had been going through. She listened without interrupting and, when I was finished, she proceeded to inform me that her ex-husband was arrested for one of the largest child pornography stings in Colorado—while they were married.

She was blindsided to learn that she was married to a man she didn't even know. A man who had been living a second life. Because of his actions and arrest, she lost many friends, her job, and had to move because strangers harassed her, convinced that she must have known what was going on. She lost the life she had known and lived for twenty years. In one day, it was all wiped away like a dream and everything changed.

In the moment after she shared her story with me, I said, "Wow, you win!"

She stopped me and said, "No, there is no winner of the pain game. We are both going through hurt. My story might sound more shocking, but that doesn't negate that you are also going through pain and hurt. Your pain is just as real as mine."

The problem is most of us react in this same way too often. We all compare, not only our pain or struggles, but also our entire lives to others', and *it's not healthy*.

Joshua Becker, author of the blog *Stop Comparing Your Life. Start Living It* encourages everyone to focus on themselves:

> ***Comparing yourself to others will always cause you to regret what you aren't, rather than allow you to enjoy life as who you are.***

He goes on to say:

> ***Celebrate who you are. There are many wonderful things about your life. You are an artist…or a businessman…or a mother…or a good listener…or a generous soul. You have much to celebrate and are entirely unique. Any comparison between you and another person is like comparing apples to oranges. They aren't living your life, you are.***

The struggles you have gone through in your life might not be as devastating as what other people have gone through, but you can't discount your pain because of that. There's no competition for who has the worst life experiences. You have your hurt, and it's real.

Of course, there are always people who have it better or worse, but comparing your pain to someone else's is dangerous. By comparing your pain and struggles to someone else's, you are denying the fact that your pain is real. You are diminishing your own pain, stating that it is not worth expressing.

Let's say you lost your job and are devastated. Another person could have lost the very same job as you, yet their circumstances in life have them feeling relieved and excited about what's to come instead of feeling anxious and scared. If two people can process the exact same experience in such different ways, then there shouldn't be comparison for "whose life is worse."

The way you process your own struggles is unique to your story. You can't compare who is processing and handling it better anymore than you can compare your life struggles to someone else's.

In 2006, I heard Aron Ralston speak at a conference about amputating his own arm after being trapped by a boulder for five days in Horseshoe Canyon in Utah. Inspired by his story, I purchased his book.

I came across Aron's book a few weeks after I met the woman in my apartment complex. I looked at the cover of the book, remembered his speech, and thought that I was pathetic for crying about my divorce when this man cut off his own arm. Then I realized, I was doing it again. I was comparing what I was going through to what he went through. I remembered what the woman had said to me, "There are no winners of the pain game."

Your pain is YOUR PAIN!

Obviously, comparing a divorce to amputating a limb is not apples to apples. I did not have to cut my arm off like Aron Ralston, but there was a part of me that felt like I lost a limb when I lost my husband. After having been with my ex-husband for twenty-three years, he had become a part of me and all that I did. Learning to live without my "ex-husband limb" was going to be hard.

Aron's presentation was not only about his experience inside that canyon, but he related what he went through to the struggles that we all have. We all have our own boulders in life. The struggles I have faced in life are real to me. My struggles are my own. I can be inspired by someone else's story, but I should use that as motivation, not as an opportunity to tear myself down and tell myself that my pain and struggles don't matter (and neither should you).

Comparing your life to others' will only cause you to question yourself rather than allow you to tend to your own wounds, process at your own pace, heal, and move forward. Your challenges in life are part of your journey. They are a component of your unique story that is not worthy of comparison. As Joshua Becker said, "They aren't living your life, you are."

Remember, **You Got This!**

Ingredient Activity

List three things that you have recently compared to someone else. Next to those, write something positive about your life.

1.

2.

3.

CHAPTER 9

IMPERMANENCE

What we think we know about the unknown is what prompts our fear.

> **impermanence**
> *noun*
> the state or fact of lasting for only a limited period of time.

Maid of Honor Speech: I met Jackie when I was fifteen. I've been with her through her first bad perm, when she failed her driving test, and when we were suspended from school for, well, let's just say, getting in trouble. I was with her through her first heartbreak, and I will never forget the night she told me he was going to marry Caleb. You two are meant for each other. I knew it from the first time I saw you together. So, let us raise a glass to Jackie and Caleb. Today is a day filled with happiness but remember, this too shall pass.

Can you imagine????

Have you ever been having the time of your life, laughing, smiling, and feeling so happy only to have someone say to you, "This too shall pass?"

Probably not!

That phrase is usually only used when you are going through a challenging time in your life. It's not something you would hear at a wedding, birthday party, or for an exciting promotion—am I right?

"This too shall pass" is a Persian phrase that reflects on the temporary nature or impermanence of anything and everything.

"This too shall pass" means that the difficult things you are facing will pass, but it also means that the amazing things you experience will pass as well. In other words: **impermanence.**

What is Impermanence?

Impermanence is the state of accepting that everything is temporary. Acceptance of impermanence is not meant to make you a "Debbie Downer," but the idea is that it allows you to cope more easily with challenging times if you can accept that life is fluid.

When you conclude that life and everything in it is not permanent (relationships, children, job, physical capabilities, financial status, etc.), then you are more likely to react gracefully when something in your life changes. Impermanence can give you hope that the painful moments won't last forever. It also can encourage you to work on being more present because you, your relationships, your job, and your mental state will not always be in a permanent state of happiness and bliss.

What Can You Gain by Learning to Accept Impermanence?

- **You accept that bad things will come to an end.**
- **You accept that good things will come to an end.**
- **You accept that ALL emotions are fluid and won't last forever.**
- **You accept that life is dynamic, not static.**

When you are happy, enjoy it! Treasure those moments and be as present as you can be. When you are hurting, feel it, acknowledge it, learn from it, and know that it won't last forever. You never know if your next moment will be a good or bad moment, but you do know that, whichever it is, it will change.

How Do You Accept Impermanence?

Well, you already have before and probably didn't even realize it.

Think back to the last time you had the cold or the flu. You didn't say to yourself, "This is it. It's been a good life. I'm dying." Okay, maybe you *felt* like that for a second, but in reality you knew it would last three to five days, and you would feel better again. That's practicing and accepting impermanence.

Embracing impermanence in my life has made me more mindful of living in the present and more emotionally grounded. It also reminds me that things will happen in life that I don't have control over, but I get to control how I to respond to them. **Synonyms you can associate with the word "uncertainty":**

- **Fear**
- **Doubt**
- **Failure**
- **Worry**
- **Confusion**
- **Uneasiness**
- **Anxiety**

A phrase that denotes the same meaning as "embrace uncertainty" is "lean into the pain." However, when most of us are uncomfortable, we want to get the hell out of Dodge, not lean in. We want out of the discomfort. But it's in those times of "embracing uncertainty" and "leaning into the pain," that we learn and grow—even though it can be hard as fuck!

All three of these phrases involve you taking a good hard look at the situation instead of doing what you want to do (run, hide, or pretend it's not happening). On a deep psychological level, we as humans *want* certainty. We want to know what our grade is going to be after the test. We want to know that we won't lose our job. We want to know that next year is going to be better than this year.

The fear of not knowing what lies ahead is difficult. We don't know what's going to happen next year, we don't know what's going to happen tomorrow. Living in fear, running, hiding, or avoiding something because we are afraid to "lean into the pain" or "embrace the uncertainty" will only heighten your anxiety. If you actively work on getting "comfortable with being uncomfortable," you will find you are leaning in more than you are running away. The key is to be comfortable with uncertainty.

Why? Because it exists. You shouldn't retreat because you were expecting a five-course gourmet meal and instead got frozen pizza. You grow and change by being exposed to uncertainty and confronting the unknown. Remember, nothing is permanent. It will change.

So How Do You Do It?

The answer to this question will be different for each of us. Some find meditation a good way to slow down and lean into pain, others prefer journal-writing or talking things through with a friend or therapist.

You can Google a million different ways to embrace uncertainty, lean into pain, or get comfortable being uncomfortable. Though there are a lot of great suggestions out there, not all of them will work for everyone. Pick and choose what works for you! However, my *one* suggestion on how to embrace uncertainly is:

When you start to get overwhelmed by the uncertainty, focus on the things you CAN control and remember that life is fluid, ever-changing, and impermanent.

You get to control how you respond in situations. When you focus on the things you CAN control, it helps you prepare for leaning into the discomfort of the uncontrollable and accepting impermanence a bit more.

Let's try our hypothetical maid of honor speech again. Picking it up from the end.

"You two are meant for each other, I knew it from the first time I saw you together.

The advice I give you today I've learned during my own journey. In my own marriage, I have learned to embrace impermanence. You will have amazing moments together, but those will pass. You will also face challenges that will pass and be replaced by happy moments once again. This journey you are on together is fluid and will be forever changing. You never know what's going to happen but embrace all of it! It's all a part of the ride you are taking together. Let us raise a glass to Jackie and Caleb!"

Remember, **You Got This!**

Ingredient Activity

List three times in your life when you felt like things weren't going to get better, but they did. For example, when you had the flu, but recovered a week later.

1.

2.

3.

CHAPTER 10

FLEXIBILITY

Flexibility is essential when you face *uncertainty*.

> **flexibility**
> *noun*
> the ability to be easily modified; willingness to change or compromise.

CHAPTER 10: FLEXIBILITY

When I was eighteen, I had my life all planned out. I was going to:

1. Go to college at the University of Kansas and graduate with a degree in psychology.
2. Get married to my high school sweetheart at twenty-five.
3. Have my first baby at twenty-six and second at twenty-eight.
4. By thirty, I would be living in Colorado with my husband and two kids all while having a successful psychology practice. I would live in my dream house and take amazing family vacations every summer.

Now for the reality check...

- ✓ Go to college at the University of Kansas and graduate with a degree in psychology.
- ✓ Get married to my high school sweetheart at twenty-five.
- ✗ Have my first baby at twenty-six and the second at twenty-eight.
- ✗ By thirty, I would be living in Colorado with my husband, two kids and have a successful psychology practice. I would be living in the house of my dreams and taking amazing family vacations every summer. (Well, I do live in Colorado, at least!)

My current life is certainly not how I thought life in my early forties would look: I'm divorced, no longer at the stable job I had for thirteen years, I rent, and I don't have children. But guess what? I am happy with where I am in my life.

I've realized that if life hurts sometimes you are probably doing it right. I wasted a full year whining and complaining about the way things "should" have gone because this was not how my life was supposed to end up. But the truth is yes it was. Because this is where I'm at right now.

Your life didn't turn out how you planned. So, it's time to write a new ending. Better yet, focus on writing the next chapter because none of us know how our stories are going to end.

It's okay to be upset that things didn't go as you intended. It's okay to be angry, ashamed, disappointed, and have mixed emotions. Then it's time to give your sauce a stir, throw in a few spices, and move forward.

It's hard work adjusting, reframing, and reorganizing your life after you had it figured out. Rather than look at restructuring as a huge chore, try viewing it as an exciting adventure into the unknown. An opportunity to redefine things in your life.

How to Start Revising Your Unexpected Next Chapter

- **Be accepting of where you are.**
  You can't rewind and you can't fast forward. THIS is where you are right now. That doesn't mean this is where you are going to stay but today this is where you are. If you don't like where you are keep working on what's next.

- **Failure isn't a bad F word.**
  You haven't failed, or maybe you have. But failure doesn't mean you ARE a failure. Failure can be viewed as growth. If you have failed at something, that's okay. Learn from it and move forward. Just because you fail at something, doesn't mean you have failed at life.

- **Be open to new things.**
  Maybe you lost your job during COVID-19 and now is the perfect time to revisit that business idea you had years ago. Perhaps you got a job offer in another state and now that you are single you accept it because you can move. Keep an open mind and be willing to shake things up a bit.

- **Be kind to yourself.**
  Don't be so hard on yourself. Even if you accept responsibility for the change in your life, stop beating yourself up. Forgive yourself if you have wronged someone else (even ask them for forgiveness if that is a part of your healing journey). Beating yourself up daily because things aren't going as you planned only hurts you in the long run. Being kind during your journey includes being kind to yourself.

- **Learn to trust.**
  Trust is very hard for many people after they have been hurt by someone or disappointed that something in their life did not turn out as planned. Trusting yourself is the first step to being able to

trust others. Trust that whatever choices you are making are a part of your process. You might make some choices that others wouldn't agree with, but right now the choices you make are a part of your process and will propel you forward in a positive direction. Trust your instincts.

- **Ask yourself what you learned.**
  I accept responsibility for everything that has happened in my life, whether it was within my control or not. I cannot change anything that has happened in my past, but I can learn from it. Life presents us with challenges from time to time, and you don't always get to choose what happens. But you *do* get to choose how you react. You can be bitter, or you can learn and grow from these experiences.

Rather than feel victimized and blame the world for how things have turned out, choose to embrace the unforeseen. It can be empowering—scary, but empowering. Remind yourself that—even when you plan out your day, your week, your year, or your life—the universe has plans of its own. How you choose to respond to life happening is what really matters. Life may not always go the way we plan it, but life happens the way it's supposed to.

Just as you do when following a recipe: you have to adjust and substitute when you are out of a specific ingredient. Having a plan for your life is great, but be flexible and adaptable as things WILL happen that are out of your control.

Remember, **You Got This!**

Ingredient Activity

List three situations that you are struggling with right now because they aren't going as you imaged they would. Next to them, list two ways you can be flexible and okay with the outcome, even if it's different than what you had planned.

1.

    1.

    2.

2.

    1.

    2.

3.

    1.

    2.

CHAPTER 11

GRATITUDE

Gratitude turns small things you take for granted into big things you cherish.

> **gratitude**
> *noun*
> the quality of being thankful; readiness to show appreciation for and to return kindness.

CHAPTER 11: GRATITUDE

Sometimes you can look back on your life and be grateful for a challenging situation because it led you to a better place. However, when you are in the moment it can be hard to be grateful. Finding gratitude during a challenging situation doesn't have to be about that specific situation, but rather finding anything in your life to be grateful for—no matter how small.

In early 2021, I was scheduled to take a trip to Florida to visit a family friend when a spring storm hit Colorado, cancelling all outbound flights. I was BUMMED to say the least! I was leaving Colorado for a few days to clear my head and warm up. Thanks stupid snowstorm!

Even though I was disappointed, I made myself a "grocery list" of some things I was grateful for which included heat, a flexible job that would let me postpone my trip for a week, and the ability to get some things organized around my house since I was snowed in. A week later, I finally arrived in Florida. Because of my trip being postponed a week, I was able to do a few things during that trip that wouldn't have happened had I arrived a week prior. In the end, I was grateful for the very snowstorm I had been cursing.

There is an amazing article by Elizabeth Heubeck where she talks about the fact that grateful people are all-around happier people. She goes on to question: what would happen if we extended the tradition of giving thanks from just one day a year to giving thanks throughout the entire year. Heubeck even touches on gratitude in the face of loss or tragedy. She cites a survey done by Christopher Peterson, PhD, a university of Michigan psychologist. Peterson conducted a survey after September 11, 2001 where he noted a surge in people feeling gratitude. But why? Peterson contributed this surge in gratitude to post-9/11 Americans having an increased sense of belonging.

But how can you do it? How do you step away from your sadness, frustration, stress, and loneliness for two seconds when you are disappointed? How do you take the time to say aloud what you are grateful for?

Five Tips for Finding Gratitude in the Thralls of Sadness, Frustration, Stress, and Loneliness

1. **Make a list.**
   Seems simple enough right? I've done this many different ways. I've sat at my desk with a journal and listed things like: my health, the roof over my head, my car, and pizza. Once, a jerk on a bike cussed me out when I was running on a trail because I had my headphones in and didn't hear him behind me. The gratitude entry for that note might have been along the lines of: "I'm grateful I had the strength to not push him off his bike!" But, in all seriousness, lists can help you visualize what you are truly grateful for.

2. **Say something (yes, actually say it aloud) that you are grateful for in that exact moment.**
   If making a whole list is too daunting, just say one thing in the moment when you feel stress or sadness creeping in. Today I said, "I am so grateful for

socks!" It's super cold outside, and my toesies are chilly. So, I'm honestly grateful I have clean socks to put on to keep me warm, because not everyone has that.

3. **Gratitude Meditation.**
   I've struggled with this one for a long time but I'm getting there and see the benefits. There are so many ways to meditate, but one I recommend if you've struggled with this in the past is Transcendental Meditation, which is more of a passive and relaxing process.

4. **Surround yourself with positive people.**
   When you are trying to be positive and have more gratitude, there is nothing worse than when Negative Nancy's try to pull you down to their level. If you are with your family and friends and are finding that it's stressful, give yourself grace to step away and take some "you" time. In that quiet time you have given yourself, try number two above.

5. **Doing good to feel good.**
   Studies show that volunteering has many positive benefits, one of which is gratitude. I used to manage 1,400 volunteers and could never get over how amazing these people were who gave so much of their free time to help a cause they were passionate about. It's certainly beneficial for the organization, but there's also a selfish component to it—a good

selfish! Volunteering also makes the volunteer feel good.

Being grateful does not mean you are forgetting your hardships or trying to push them under the rug. Being truly thankful is the ability to appreciate what you do have. It's not suggesting that being grateful means everything in the world is great. You have to open your eyes, your heart, and your mind to even the little things that make your heart smile.

Remember, **You Got This!**

Ingredient Activity

Try practicing gratitude every day for a month. Download my free gratitude journal at this website: https://goodthingsaregonnacome.com/gratitude-workbook/

CHAPTER 12

CHOICES

You don't always get to choose what life throws at you, but you always get to choose how you respond.

> **choice**
> *noun*
> an act of making a decision when faced with two or more possibilities.

CHAPTER 12: CHOICES

Do you remember in grade school when there were two captains who picked the teams for kickball? You were either the kid that got picked first because of your mad left foot that sent the ball flying into the outfield, or you were like me, hoping to be on Jenny's team but ending up the last pick on John's team. You didn't get to choose who picked you, but you did have a choice on how you handled being selected last. You could have:

1. Faked an injury, so you had to sit out.
2. Pouted and trudged onto the field, half-assing your effort in the game.
3. Gave it your all and made Jenny regret not picking you after you won the game with a home run!

While people may think that sometimes they have no choice in life, I beg to differ. All of us have choices, and we exercise them every day, every minute, and every second.

After we are born (which is pretty much the only choice we have no say in), there are things that happen to us that we wouldn't necessarily choose. But we do get to choose how we respond to the outcomes that are made for us. We have control of our lives. Maybe not control over everything that is presented to us, but we decide how we respond to life. You cannot control the world, but you can control how you react to various situations.

Six months before I lost my job in 2018, I was unhappy and contemplating a career change. However, I was already going through a divorce, the loss of my beloved nineteen-year-old dog, and dealing with my own health issues. Although I was displeased with my work life, I had been at my job thirteen years. It was a constant that I knew and was comfortable with. I decided that it was best to stay at my job for the time being.

However, life had other plans. Although I preferred to stay, that choice was taken away from me. The loss of my job presented me with a series of other choices. I didn't decide to leave my job, but now I got to choose how I was going to respond.

- Do I look at this as a blessing because I was unhappy anyway?
- Do I go back and work for another company or organization that can easily dismiss me after thirteen years of hard work and dedication?
- Do I throw caution to the wind and try something new that actually makes me happy?

I don't know how long I would have stayed in my job if I hadn't been let go. Yes, I was unhappy, but having gone through so many other changes, I liked knowing there was a constant in my life. I didn't choose to leave, but because of the choices I made after I lost my job, I am happier than I was with that job.

Sometimes you may not recognize that you have a choice because your circumstances are overwhelming. They overpower you to the point where life looks like a series of constraints, and you fell as if you don't have any control over what you're facing.

CHAPTER 12: CHOICES

Life is a series of choices and most are based on two things: fear (escape-based) or love (target-based). Often, we choose fear over love. Nearly 80% of our choices are fear-based:

- We fear making the wrong choice.
- We fear the unknown.
- We fear rejection.
- We fear failure.

People frequently complain about the way their life is going over and over like a broken record (I have been there). Yet, if you ask them what they have been doing about it to make a change, they say, "nothing," or come up with reasons to justify why they haven't been doing anything differently. It basically sums up to "I don't have a choice."

I accept responsibility for everything that has happened in my life, whether it was within my control or not. I have the choice to take charge and alter my life recipe by using the seasonings that, maybe, weren't my first preference but are available for me to cook with. I can rise above my constraints to create what I want. Over the past three years, life has presented me with a lot of challenges that I might not have chosen to happen, but I got to choose how I reacted to them.

If you keep thinking that you have no control over your life, that's exactly how it will remain. You will always be the person who is powerless. When you recognize that your life is *your life*, and everything you do is a choice that *you* make is when you will see a change. Rather than blame your external environment for your struggles, choose to become proactive in your own life. Rather than feeling victimized, gain power over circumstances by choosing to respond with love (target-based) rather than fear (escape-based).

Are you finding it difficult to make a decision in life right now? Perhaps life threw you a curve ball and now you have to choose how to respond. As you figure out your next step, ask yourself: Is this an escape-based choice or a target-based choice?

No matter how difficult things may seem, remember you always have a choice.

If you want to stay in bed today and eat potato chips because life presented you with a bad situation, that is your choice and completely understandable. Being sad is a part of any healing process. However, if today is a day you choose to get out of bed and be metaphorical Jenny's pick on the kickball team, then I hope you choose to give it your all and kick ass!

Remember, **You Got This!**

Ingredient Activity

List a time when you didn't have a choice in the matter, and you wanted to stomp your feet and throw a temper tantrum. Looking back at that situation, what was a choice you made that helped you move forward?

If you look back and see that you could have made a different choice, what would it have been?

CHAPTER 13

FAST-FORWARD

If you fast-forward through the bad times, you'll also miss the good times.

> **fast-forward**
> *verb*
> move speedily forward in time when considering or dealing with something over a period.

CHAPTER 13: FAST-FORWARD

How many times have you wished that you could hit the fast-forward button in your life? Think back to your childhood. You thought that if you skipped an entire week in December, then Christmas would arrive more quickly (or maybe that was just me?).

There's an Adam Sandler movie, *Click,* where he hits a magical fast-forward button through all the hard parts of his life, such as a fight with his wife. On the surface, the ability to fast-forward our lives, especially when pain is involved, seems like a great idea. But as the movie continues, Adam Sandler realizes that all of those hard parts of his life that he was skipping over also caused him to skip over the good.

It sucks to admit, but you don't get to experience the good without the shit that accompanies life. Our journey is full of ups and downs, bumps and bruises, love and loss. You can't have the good without the bad. You need to do your best to work through the bad and learn from your mistakes, so you can endure and overcome.

During the early stages of my divorce, I felt like I was trapped in a tunnel. Seeing a light at the end of the tunnel, I wanted to fast-forward to get to the other end—but it seemed impossible. It felt like I would take one step toward the light, but then another shitty thing would happen and I would take two steps back. However, something deep inside kept telling me that the only way out was through the tunnel.

Although we really want to, if we all fast-forwarded through the hard times, what would we actually learn? It's these difficult times that teach us something. They suck and they are hard, and the natural reaction most of us have is to run away—or fast-forward.

I have never experienced drug or alcohol detoxing, but have had friends and family go through it so I have some understanding. You experience nausea, shakes, sweats, anxiety, vomiting, insomnia, and the list goes on. Who wouldn't want to fast-forward through that? But, if it wasn't so intense, so awful, and so miserable that it burned that experience into their brains, there's a higher likelihood of addicts going back to their old ways.

They need to remember the detox experience, the discomfort, and pain, so they don't start using again. There's no fast-forward button. They go through the experience to get to the other side, to get clean and sober, so they can hopefully stay that way.

You can relate this to your life. The deaths, the breakups, the losses, the (fill in the blank) that hurt you. It's that pain that will make you stronger. It SUCKS at times, *I know*. But, unfortunately, it's a part of life.

Take a minute to think of some strong people that you know. People who have struggled, gone through heartache, loss, and pain. The strongest people we know have not been given an easy life on a silver platter. They have learned to create happiness by walking through their pain. Walking through their tunnel to get to the other side.

The way out of your pain is always through, and you *will* get through it. Don't be afraid of feeling the pain. The pain is going to change you. It's going to make you stronger.

Life is going to suck at times, but you will get there one day at a time. Once you get through this tunnel, there will be another that will start to boil at some point, but one tunnel at a time.

CHAPTER 13: FAST-FORWARD

Because you got through the first tunnel, hopefully you will remember what helped you and what didn't so you can get through any new dark tunnels more quickly in the future.

It's going to take time, and you will get there at your own pace. At some point, you might find yourself standing still and not taking any steps forward or backward. On those days, take a moment to look around, take in what you see, and try to be grateful for those things. You can take a step forward tomorrow.

It's long, it's dark, it's scary, and (some days) it seems like an impossible task—but you *can* do it. You aren't alone.

Remember, **You Got This!**

Ingredient Activity

Recall a moment in the past year that you wanted to fast-forward. List three positive things that you learned from that experience and how it made you stronger.

1.

2.

3.

CHAPTER 14

BE KIND

A gift you can give for free...
kindness.

kindness
noun
the quality of being **friendly, generous, and considerate.**

I was once at a grocery store, standing in line with about thirty-forty items in my cart when I noticed the woman behind me had only a Diet Pepsi and a bag of chips. I insisted she go in front of me. She smiled and thanked me as she was checked out in a flash.

Another time I was at the grocery store, I had a full cart and noticed that the woman behind me had maybe five to ten items. But that time, I pretended as if I didn't see her and unloaded my cart onto the conveyer belt. As I headed out of the store, I felt like shit!

These were nearly identical situations, but in one I acted with kindness and in the other I didn't. There's no rule saying you have to let someone with fewer items go in front of you in line, but my actions the second time still don't sit right with me. I know that the first situation made me feel a lot better about myself.

Sometimes It's Easier to Be Unkind

Although preaching kindness is great, sometimes it's really hard to be kind—especially if you are having a shitty day! Let's face it, it's often easier to be unkind, particularly when we are not mentally or emotionally in a great place and we feel like the world is against us. Everyone is entitled to express what they are feeling, but that doesn't mean at the cost of hurting others or yourself.

If you are having a bad/sad/stressful day, you have every right to feel your emotions. But being unkind to others (or yourself) doesn't serve you in the long run. Humans are hard-wired for compassion; it's deep inside all of us and we should all try to tap into that as much as we can. Advances in neuroscience have shown that the human brain has neural networks that are hard-wired with the ability to share the experiences of others.

It's unrealistic however, to think that you will never say another unkind thing or act unkindly to another person. But keep in mind, being kind actually takes less work than being unkind. We each have the capability to be kind and make the world a better place than it was when we woke up. The truth is, being kind actually increases our own level of happiness. There are hundreds of websites out there that suggest ways to spread kindness:

- **Buy a stranger's coffee.**
- **Give someone a compliment.**
- **Hold the door for someone.**
- **Leave a generous tip when eating out.**
- **Donate your time.**
- **Bring your neighbor cookies or a meal.**
- **Smile or say hello.**

The list of kind things you can do goes on and on—but I think most of us know what constitutes as being kind to someone. I have my own "kindness compass" that I use to spread kindness, but no matter what good deed you choose to exercise, I have four tips for you to practice when being kind to others (and to yourself).

Kindness Tips

1. Act with good intent
If you are only being kind to receive gratitude, you're doing it for the wrong reason. You might be kind to someone and get the opposite response than what you are expecting. However, if your intent is to be kind (no matter the outcome), that is key. You can't control others' reactions, and some people are just jerks.

2. Be authentic
Authenticity is about confidence and staying true to yourself. Be *genuine* with your kindness.

3. Try to see things from another's perspective
You don't know what someone else is going through. We all have our own battles. Let's say the car on the road in front of you is driving ten miles under the speed limit. You're frustrated and honk. When that does nothing, you swerve past and flip them off. Little did you know that was a sixteen-year-old driving to school for the first time without an adult in the car.

This can go for yourself, as well. Don't beat yourself up for sleeping in an extra hour instead of getting your workout in. You were being kind to yourself by giving yourself some much needed sleep to get through the busy day ahead of you. You can always work out later tonight or tomorrow.

4. Breathe
If you find yourself getting angry, overwhelmed, frustrated, or wanting to be unkind—pause and breathe. This has been

my saving grace many, many days. Take a moment, take a deep breath.

As you are navigating your own personal challenges in life, you might not list being kind to *others* as a top priority in your life recipe. However the reality is, it does feel good when you practice kindness.

You never know how grateful someone might be if you let them go in front of you at the grocery store, and how healing it can be for you!

Remember, **You Got This!**

Ingredient Activity

List three random acts of kindness that you have done in the past year.

1.

2.

3.

List two things you could do this week to show kindness to a stranger or someone you know.

1.

2.

CHAPTER 15

QUITTING

There is a difference between giving up and knowing when to walk away.

quit
verb
to stop, cease, or discontinue.

I was sixteen-years-old, standing in the outfield as I saw the ball soaring towards me. I put my glove up, closed my eyes, and hoped the ball would land in my glove verses the top of my head. Well, it hit me right in the head! I'm kidding, I got lucky and caught it!

Growing up in a small town it was the assumption that when spring came around you would go out for a sport. I hurt myself in track the previous year so I thought, "Sure, I can play softball."

I took it seriously and practiced extremely hard, even on weekends with my dad because I wanted to impress the coaches and my teammates. I have good eye-hand coordination, I can run, I can throw, but no matter how hard I practiced, something didn't click with me…I wasn't good.

I began dreading practices and hitting a fastball off of some of the girls that went on to play college ball. Let's just say when I was up to bat I often heard, "STRIKE THREE." The truth was, I didn't like it.

I was complaining to my sister about my frustrations and she said to me, "Stop your whining, why don't you quit." It hadn't even occurred to me, was that really an option?

If I quit what would people think? What would they say? Would my dad be disappointed? Would I be disappointed in myself?

After contemplating my options, I concluded that I had given it all I had but had to accept I wasn't good at softball. So, I did it—I quit the team. It was as if a huge weight had been lifted off my shoulders. I was so happy with my decision, it allowed me to focus on my passions of singing and dancing and never regretted it.

CHAPTER 15: QUITTING

Quitting is often seen as a sign of weakness, a lack of aptitude, or a failure. If you can't cut it, you quit. If it's too hard, you quit. If you're not good enough at it, you quit.

Think about the couple that no longer communicates. They are more like roommates than lovers and have grown apart over the years. They have tried couples therapy and have actually put in the work, but they are both still unhappy. What are they supposed to do? Stay in a loveless, miserable marriage because society frowns on divorce? Quitting is usually painted as a negative attribute—in relationships, in work, and in life, "not giving up" is considered a respected skill.

In 2018, I trained for four months for the Denver Century Ride, my first 100-mile bike ride. The weekend before the race, I caught a nasty cold and woke up sick as a dog! I had a fever, awful congestion, and felt like I had been hit by a truck. On the morning of the race, I had two choices:

1. Bow out and try again next month.

2. Suck it up (I had trained four months for this!).

Since I am a bit stubborn, I opted for option two. Eight hours later, I finished my Century Ride. However, the next morning I was in the hospital being administered fluids, put on oxygen, and diagnosed with walking pneumonia. Looking back, this was probably one of those times I should have quit!

The kicker? I wasn't even happy that I finished! I was upset with my time since I wasn't able to ride as hard as I knew I could have had I been healthy instead. I didn't even have fun *and* ended up with a hospital bill because I was too proud to quit and simply try again next month.

I believe in working hard on relationships, working hard at your job, and working hard in life overall. But, sometimes, it's okay to throw in the towel. However, I don't believe in quitting because something is difficult. Life is hard, period! Don't quit just because it's hard:

- **Quit because it sucks.**
- **Quit because you've lost your passion.**
- **Quit because you're unhappy.**
- **Quit because it it's unhealthy for you physically and/or mentally.**
- **Quit because it's fiscally irresponsible.**
- **Quit because you want more.**
- **Quit because you deserve more.**

Don't be bullied by society, friends, family, or your own ego into staying in a job you hate, hanging onto a business that is putting you in debt, pushing through the pain in that race and risking an injury, or not saying goodbye to a relationship that is no longer healthy for you.

Throughout our lives, we have been told that quitting is only for losers. But I believe nothing is further from the truth. How and why you quit shows your true strength. Self-preservation is not selfish. True winners confront quitting with grace. I encourage you to work hard and push yourself. You are capable of so many things. But on the flip side, don't be afraid to throw in the towel. Listen to yourself. Only you know what is best for you, this is your recipe!

Remember, **You Got This!**

Ingredient Activity

Name a time in life when you thought about quitting but pushed yourself and found it was worth it in the end.

Name a time when you wanted to quit but didn't, and you regretted it. How would things have been different if you would have quit instead?

CHAPTER 16
BOUNDARIES

An absence of boundaries welcomes an absence of respect.

boundary
noun
something that indicates or fixes a limit or extent

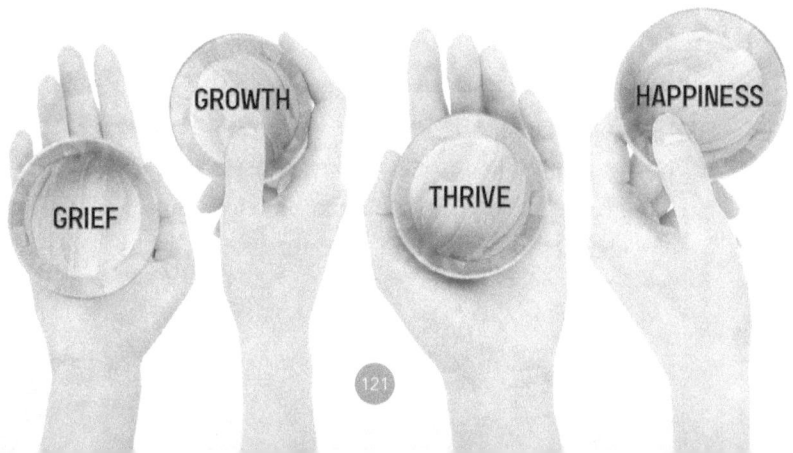

CHAPTER 16: BOUNDARIES

I started a new job when I was twenty-four, and (not to toot my own horn) I was a rock star! Actually, you know what, screw that—TOOT, TOOT! Because I was *really* good at that job! I proved myself to my boss, and he quickly gave me more and more to do, which I loved!

I was promoted in less than a year and had two more promotions the following year. I was one of the youngest directors across the country for this nationwide organization. As my job responsibilities increased, I found that I was taking on more, and I never said no to my boss.

Four people were laid off due to restructuring, and I was expected to absorb all of their job responsibilities. After three years I was burnt out. Although I loved my job, I was mentally exhausted. If I had known the phrase, "personal boundaries" at that point, I might have had a conversation with my boss rather than find a new job.

Personal boundaries are important for us to have—not just at work, but in all areas of our lives. Our boundaries are limits we decide for how our co-workers, bosses, friends, family, and partners can treat us.

I struggled for years on how to express healthy boundaries. I lived my life to please others. I never said no—not wanting to offend anyone—even if it wasn't in my best interest and made me uncomfortable. I wasn't even a fan of the word "boundaries." It felt like a buzzword that people used as an excuse to be an ass when they didn't want to do something. But now, I find boundaries necessary. And I like talking to my clients about how to practice implementing them when it's a new concept.

What are Boundaries, Anyway?

Personal boundaries are the limits you decide work for you on how people can treat you, how they can behave around you, and what they can expect from you. Boundaries are the standards you set about your expectations, accessibility, and energy. They are drawn from your core beliefs, your perspective, your opinions, and your values.

If this concept is hard to understand, think of other boundaries. State lines, fences, or a line in the sand. Boundaries convey how you feel, prevent you from over-committing, and guide others in knowing how you want to be treated.

Why Do I Need Boundaries?

- **Do you feel like people take advantage of you?**
- **Do you hate drama but seem to always be surrounded by it?**
- **Do you feel like you are constantly having to "save" people or be the "nice one" because that's "who you are?"**
- **Do you feel like it's your job to fix other people's problems?**
- **Do you feel like you have to explain or defend yourself for things that aren't your fault?**

If you answered yes to anything above, you probably have a little work to do on setting personal boundaries. There is a great Boundary Checklist on www.makingmidlifematter.com that I love. The suggestions that were most impactful for me were:

> *Healthy Boundary: Acknowledging what you are feeling*
>
> *Unhealthy Boundary: Ignoring your feelings*

Boundaries are a form of self-care. If you don't set healthy boundaries, you are setting yourself up to feel used, overworked, stressed, frustrated, and unhappy. Having boundaries isn't bitchy, it's actually an act of self-love.

How Do You Set Boundaries?

1. Define
Tune into your feelings and ask yourself, "What are my limits? What is something that I don't want to tolerate in my life?" Think of a situation where you felt like you didn't set boundaries. What happened in that situation? What feelings did you have? What would you do differently? How would you have felt if you had expressed your boundaries in said situation?

2. Communicate
Learning to say no can be very hard, especially if it's not the way you were raised. It's not going to feel natural at first and, as with many things, it will take practice. Saying no is

okay. But remember, when someone says no to you, that's okay, too.

Setting boundaries with a stranger, is certainly an easier place to start than setting boundaries with someone you care about. For example, you can walk away from a conversation where your co-worker lights up a cigarette because you don't want to be around cigarette smoke. Or you can start by solidifying your boundaries concerning food if you are gluten intolerant and on a first date. Would you order a meal that "might" have gluten in it, so you didn't offend your date? I'm guessing you would enforce your food boundary, so you didn't end up in the bathroom all night!

If you are not familiar with setting boundaries in your life, start small. A great way to strengthen your confidence is to start with a non-threatening boundary that doesn't feel overwhelming. Starting small allows you to slowly build upon your confidence to tackle more challenging boundaries.

Don't forget, other people have boundaries too, and they will most likely express those to you at some point. Just as you want others to respect your boundaries, respecting others' boundaries is just as important.

Remember, **You Got This!**

Ingredient Activity

Recall a time when you should have set a boundary and didn't. How would you handle that situation differently today by enforcing your boundaries?

What is one boundary you could set today?

CHAPTER 17

FORGIVENESS

Forgiving yourself is the ultimate forgiveness.

forgive
verb
to stop feeling angry or resentful for an offense, flaw, or mistake.

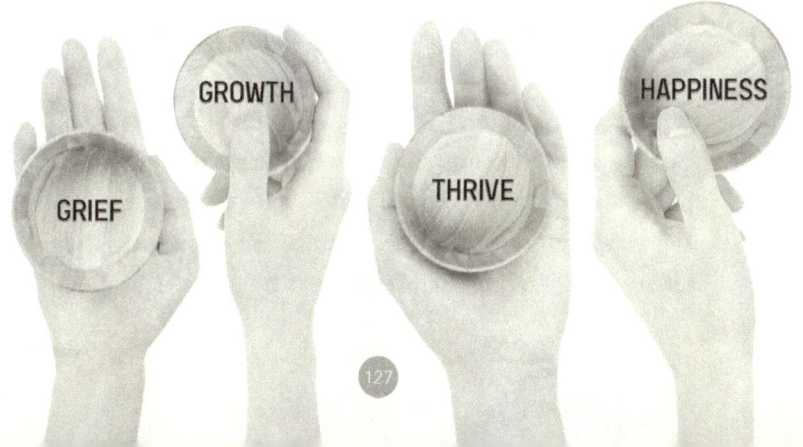

CHAPTER 17: FORGIVENESS

"Shrimp!"

"Fatty!"

"I hate you!"

"Yeah, well, I hate you!"

My recollection of a spat between my brother and I when I was eight and he was eleven. We did NOT get along growing up. We picked on each other almost daily, partially due to the fact that he was the only boy with three sisters. My brother was small and thin for his age, and I was (as I like to say) stocky. I'm pretty sure we weighed the same, or I might have even outweighed him by a few pounds.

The name-calling between my brother and I affected us both—far more deeply than two children can understand in the moment. Now, my brother and I are both grown adults with a great relationship. When we think back on the name-calling we did when we were young, we both chuckle. But then, I think about how awful I felt about those words I said to him all those years ago. Even though we have both since apologized and forgiven each other, for years, this past behavior still ate at me.

There is a lot of controversy on whether or not forgiveness is necessary when you are healing. Many claim we need to forgive to heal. We've all done things in our lives that we wish we could take back, but do we need to forgive and forget?

You get to choose if you forgive others. I'm not telling you that you should or shouldn't forgive someone for something they have done to you or that has affected you in a negative way. That is very personal choice. For some, forgiving is a way of liberating themselves, and it facilitates healing.

However, others can't bring themselves to forgive as they don't feel that it brings them any closure. Those people are being honest with themselves and honoring their feelings, and that's okay.

While I have my own thoughts on forgiving others, I do believe that for *me* to fully heal inside, grow, and be the best version of myself possible—forgiveness is necessary. If I am harboring ill feelings toward others who may or may not still be in my life, those feelings are not serving me in a positive way.

However, this chapter is not about forgiving others, it's about **self-forgiveness**, which often can be a hell of a lot harder than forgiving someone else who has hurt you. During my journey, I focused a lot on forgiving others, but I forgot there was one other person in my life whom I hadn't forgiven for things she did—me.

Let's remember that forgiveness doesn't mean forgetting. Forgiveness means that you've made peace with the pain, and you are ready to let it go.

Self-forgiveness is not about letting yourself off the hook. It's about accepting what has happened, acknowledging that you can't change the past, learning from your experience, and moving forward.

Dr. Laura Schlessinger suggests that there are four stages of forgiveness:

1. Responsibility
2. Remorse
3. Repair
4. Restore (or don't repeat)

My interpretation of her stages:

1. OWN THAT SHIT!
Even if you try to pretend the situation or incident never happened, it's not going away. Face what you have done. This is a hard stage because you might try to rationalize or justify your actions. Even if there might be a tiny bit of justification, you should do your best to set that aside and sit with what you did or said.

2. FEEL IT
Once you fully accept responsibility, guilt and shame can enter, which might make you want to start rationalizing or justifying again. This stage can be emotional, bringing up feelings of worthlessness or depression. But the guilt is natural.

3. SAY/WRITE IT
Saying you are sorry isn't always an option, but if you can—do. If the person/people whom you hurt is/are no longer in your life, write a letter to them (even if they will never see it).

4. LEARN YOUR LESSON
We all make mistakes in life. Try your best to figure out what you learned from this experience, so you don't repeat it.

I'm not telling you that you need to forgive someone in your life for a wrongdoing. What I am suggesting is that if there is something you're holding onto that you haven't forgiven yourself for, maybe now is the time to acknowledge it and start that forgiveness process. Self-forgiveness is not something you do for others—it's something you do for yourself.

- **Self-forgiveness doesn't mean excusing your action.**
- **Self-forgiveness doesn't mean never thinking about the situation again.**
- **Self-forgiveness doesn't mean forgetting the incident ever happened.**

By forgiving yourself, you are taking responsibility for your actions. But self-forgiveness is easier said than done. Being able to forgive yourself requires compassion, empathy, patience, and understanding. Forgiveness is a gift you give yourself.

Remember, **You Got This!**

Ingredient Activity

Think of a time in the past where you wronged someone else.

You can't change what has happened, but you can work on forgiving yourself. List three ways you could start by forgiving yourself. (Example: write a letter to the person who you want to forgive you even if you don't intend on sending it.)

CHAPTER 18
HEAD-HEART-GUT

You know your truth by the way you feel.

intuition
noun
the ability to understand something immediately without the need for conscious reasoning.

CHAPTER 18: HEAD-HEART-GUT

Imagine you're on trial for murder, and you're innocent. The prosecuting attorney does not have evidence, and things seem to be going in your favor. As the jury heads back to deliberate the evidence, which implies you are innocent, one of the jurors exclaims, "I know there seems to be reasonable doubt, but my gut is telling me she is guilty."

Do you really want your fate to be decided upon because of someone's gut feeling?

Your heart leads you with love, your mind tries to keep you safe, and your gut is the deep-down feeling that you can't shake! So what do you listen to when you are trying to make a big decision in life?

Think of a decision that you are currently struggling with. If someone told you: you have to make a decision in the next five seconds, or I'm going to push you off this cliff—what are you going to go with? Your head, your heart, or your gut?

Your heart can encourage you to take chances. Without taking chances in life, growth is impossible. But sometimes, when we listen to the heart we ignore important facts and irresponsibility can override sensible decisions. The heart can often be naïve, casting off rational thinking.

Your head can anticipate consequences that your heart may downplay or overlook. Yet the mind can also be a cynic, serving up self-doubt and skepticism that may keep you from living a life filled with passion and adventure. More often than hearing the advice of "go with your heart or head," I hear the phrase, "Trust your gut." But should you?

Gut instinct or intuition is believed to be an immediate understanding of the situation from somewhere deep inside yourself. It's as if you know something, but you can't explain how. However, making a big life decision—not based on facts but on something inside yourself—can be scary.

Heart-head-gut conflicts can feel paralyzing. If you wait too long to make a decision, the opportunity might pass. But if you rush in too soon without weighing all the pros and cons, you could overlook vital information.

My opinion (and really, an opinion is all anyone can offer on this topic because there's no scientific proof that listening to any one of the three will lead to the best outcome) is to listen to all three. They might not be in sync, but breakdown what they're telling you.

- **Make a list. Write down your doubts.**
- **Write about the situation you're facing. Keep your notes to *just* the facts.**
- **List the pros and cons of making the choice your heart is telling you to go with. Then, do the same for the head and the gut.**
- **Ask yourself some hard questions. Why is my heart telling me to make this choice? What is causing me to think this way? If I was helping a friend through this, what advice would I give them?**

When you are stuck in a heart-head-gut conflict, perhaps the answer is *not* to choose one of those three and instead, order the metaphorical Neapolitan option by taking a little of the best each has to offer. You don't know how everything will turn out, but at least you will be clear on *why* you made the choice you did.

Remember, **You Got This!**

Ingredient Activity

Write down a decision you're struggling with right now.

Use the form below to list out facts and pros/cons about your situation.

PROS	CONS

FACTS
1.
2.
3.
4.
5.

CHAPTER 19

MINDSET

The power of the mind is limitless.

> **mindset**
> *noun*
> a collection of thoughts and beliefs that shape a person's habits.

One day, a professor entered his classroom and asked his students to prepare for a surprise test. They all waited anxiously at their desks for the exam to begin. The professor handed out the exams with the text facing down, as usual. Once he handed them all out, he asked the students to turn over the papers.

To everyone's surprise, there were no questions—just a black dot in the center of the paper. The professor, seeing the expression on everyone's faces, told them the following:

"I want you to write about what you see there."

The students, confused, got started on the inexplicable task. At the end of the class, the professor took all the exams and read each one of them aloud to the students. All of them defined the black dot, trying to explain its position in the center of the sheet.

After all the answers had been read, the professor explained:

"I'm not going to grade you on this. I just wanted to give you something to think about. No one wrote about the white part of the paper. Everyone focused on the black dot—and the same thing happens in our lives. We focus only on the black dot—the health issues that bother us, the money we don't have, the

complicated relationship with a family member, or the way a friend has disappointed us."

"The dark spots are very small when compared to everything we have in our lives, but they are the ones that pollute our minds. Take your eyes away from the black dots in your lives. Enjoy each one of your blessings, each moment that life gives you. Be happy and live a life filled with love!" –Author Unknown

Our mindset is our mental approach to life based on our experiences, our environment, our education, and the ideas and beliefs we have learned from the people around us. Neuro-Linguistic Programming (NLP) is an awareness of the mind, not the brain. It's a way of shifting your mindset. NLP operates through the conscious use of language to bring about changes in your thoughts and behavior. Little did I know that I was using an NLP technique twenty years prior to become a certified practitioner.

The first house I purchased with my ex-husband was a 1960s ranch style house in East Lawrence, Kansas that needed a great deal of updating. Before we moved in, we decided to paint the entire house. I spent five hours of one day painting the entire kitchen. As I was wrapping up, I saw a spot in the corner that I'd missed. I moved my stepstool over, touched up the spot, and stepped down. But I missed the bottom step, and my foot landed right in the five-gallon bucket of paint—in my brand new tennis shoes.

"Shit!"

Tears pooled in my eyes because I was pissed. I had just ruined my shoes and had no idea how I was going to get out of this situation without making a huge mess. Then, I took a deep breath and looked at the situation from a different perspective, realizing how much worse the situation could have been.

Without knowing it, I was shifting my mindset.

There are many different NLP techniques you can use when you're working on shifting your mindset: techniques to assist with your professional career, techniques to assist with fears and phobias, and techniques to assist with anxiety. The two I find the most helpful when working on transforming yourself after a challenging life decision are:

1. Anchoring

This is one of the most common NLP techniques. The objective of this technique is to prompt positive responses by associating a particular mental and emotional state to your anchor.

Anchoring is linking external triggers to internal responses. For example, when you see a stop sign, you know you need to put your foot on the break and stop.

It's used to help modify mental triggers that cause you to experience unpleasant emotions due to a past event. Just as your mind can be triggered by past trauma, you can program your mind with healthy triggers that help you feel calm and in control.

2. Reframing

This technique involves choosing your response to a situation by changing the context. Changing the frame of an experience can have a major influence on how you perceive, interpret and react to that experience.

The purpose of reframing is to help modify perception and have you look at your experiences from a different perspective or frame (like I did with the bucket of paint). It's about editing the negative emotions associated with the frames. When recalling a traumatic event (such as a divorce), certain parts of your brain respond to that painful emotion. Reframing teaches you that the nature of that emotion isn't fixed, and you can break those patterns.

Teaching your brain new ways of responding to negative thoughts doesn't stop the negative thought, but it reduces the intensity of the feelings associated with the thought. These techniques are how I overcame my divorce and my job loss, and I continue to use them in many areas of my life.

It's important to note however, implementing these techniques isn't a "one and done" and change doesn't happen overnight. As with anything in life, when you want to see results it takes consistency, practice, and a willingness to put in the effort to see sustainable change. No one can do it for you.

People with the determination to shift their mindset and accept that setbacks are a part of life are more likely to:

- **Put in more effort to keep moving forward.**
- **Welcome lifelong learning.**
- **Embrace the unknown.**
- **View challenges life presents them with in a more optimistic way.**
- **Believe in themselves.**

Remember, **You Got This!**

Ingredient Activity

Anchoring: Recall a time when you were happy. Try to remember how you felt during this time. Tap on your leg very softly when you recreate this image (a very gentle, repetitive tap on your leg). Keep thinking of this moment as you tap for about 60 seconds.

By doing this you are setting up a stimulus response pattern, so YOU have control over the way you want to feel when you need to. You are beginning to condition yourself and create an anchor. The next time you have negative thoughts or an increase in anxiety, you can use this anchor (by tapping on your knee) to induce a new frame of mind and emotion.

Reframing: What is a negative thought that you have been having over and over during your challenging transition? For example: if you recently lost your job, what is a re-occurring negative thought associated with that? List three positive things that are associated with this experience that have been challenging for you. You may have to think on this for a while, but get creative with the positives you can see.

(Example: You now have the ability to look for a job that will give you more of a work/life balance or pays better).

1.

2.

3.

COOK
TWEAK YOUR RECIPE

To adjust your life in small but meaningful ways.
Tweak daily, tweak often.

> **tweak**
> *verb*
> improve (a mechanism or system) by making fine adjustments to it.

I used to love sweets (remember butter and sugar?), but that changed. I love salty now. There might have been a time when I ordered French fries for dessert as an adult, don't judge! Some people like a little more spice, some like sweet, some salty, and that can change as they age.

Now here is the fun part! Wait, there are fun parts of transforming your life while you're navigating a challenging transition? Okay, well *fun* might be overexaggerating, but I like to think of it as *empowering* because this is all you. No one gets to tell you how to create your own recipe.

Have you ever been to a food tasting? You're given a lot of different options because the vendors know there will be some things you like and some you won't. That's the same with life. You get to change up your seasonings and tweak your life recipe to fit YOU! As you begin to incorporate the spices from these chapters into your life, be open to the idea that you can change things any time you need to!

Let's say you've been practicing self-care and love spending every Thursday morning taking a walk with your friend. But after a few months you need a change. That's okay! Be honest and tell her you need to change it up! Transformation is not a "one and done" thing, it's ever changing.

As you navigate this next chapter in your life, certain things are going to work for now, but you might (most likely will) need to adjust and change them as your life continues to unfold. Our tastes in food change as we experience challenges in life. We all have our own ways of responding and coping, which can change. Do what feels right for you and don't feel locked into a choice or decision.

That's the best part about life, you can change it up. You get to season to YOUR taste!

COOK
CONCLUSION

Chop, Sauté, Sear, Cook, Bake, Boil, Grill...
whatever you choose.

Read self-help books or don't.
Listen to podcasts or don't.
Go to therapy or don't.
Surround yourself with friends or don't.

This is *your* life recipe. You get to choose what will work for you as you transform yourself. Only you will know what resonates with you.

However, I encourage you to try a lot of different things to *see what sticks*. Remember, it takes work to transform yourself (your body and your mind). In the same way that you can't expect to have pasta boil if you don't turn on the stove, you also can't expect to see results if you do nothing to propel yourself forward.

Work doesn't have to mean that you spend two hours a day reading self-help books, schedule outings with your friends three times a week, or journal every day. Work means putting in the effort to thrive. Take it slow. Don't

CONCLUSION

try and do it all at once and overload yourself. The pain or struggle won't pass any faster, and you'll most likely overwhelm yourself.

Remember, time is a part of your healing process. But time only heals if you move along with it. You can't fast-forward through it. You have to **go** through it to **grow** through it.

No one can fix those broken, hurt, tired, sad, overwhelmed, and scared pieces inside of you. There are tools out there to help guide you, but you have to pick and choose what's going to work for you. We all go through our own personal struggles and our own personal experiences.

Even though you know you aren't the only person who has gone through a particular situation, when you are in the thick of it, you can still feel alone. Reading self-help books can give you ideas on what steps to take, but YOU have to choose what works best for you. Your therapist or coach can give you homework to make a list of things that will make you happy, but you still have to make your list.

You may have the support and encouragement of others, but this is YOUR journey, your story, and you get to create your own life recipe. No one can create it for you, ONLY YOU can do that. And you also get to tweak it when things start to "taste" bland.

I hope this book has given you a slightly different perspective on how to approach transformation after shit hits the fan in your life. If you don't have the energy to put in the work today, that's okay. Take a breath and try tomorrow, but don't give up. Keep working because you have an amazing next chapter to start living.

I have put in the effort to thrive. It hasn't been an easy road, but I have created my own life recipe that I love—but I am still (and will forever be) tweaking my seasonings, and I encourage you to do the same.

Season to taste my friend—*Buon Appetito!*

Remember, **You Got This!**

NUTRITIONAL FACTS
ENCOURAGEMENT

- I encourage you to grieve the loss that you are experiencing and allow yourself to feel the feelings associated with each stage.
- I encourage you to define what is important to you in all types of relationships in your life and to not cling to relationships that no longer serve you.
- I encourage you to love your body and listen to its needs.
- I encourage you to not let others tell you that what you are feeling is *not* okay.
- I encourage you to find what self-care means to you and do something for yourself each day.
- I encourage you to try journaling, then stop if it's not your jam.
- I encourage you to stop comparing your life, your body, or your story to others.
- I encourage you to enjoy those amazing moments you experience, knowing that life is filled with both good and bad. Remembering life is fluid.
- I encourage you to be flexible with the small things in life, which will help you be flexible with the big things in life.
- I encourage you to find things that you are grateful for each day.

- I encourage you to choose positivity when you respond to a situation that is out of your control.
- I encourage you to walk through the tunnel. You will have to go through it to get to the other side.
- I encourage you to be kind. It will make you feel better.
- I encourage you to quit something that is no longer serving you.
- I encourage you to enforce your boundaries for your mental health. If you haven't identified them yet, I encourage you to start making a list.
- I encourage you to forgive yourself for something you are hanging onto.
- I encourage you to tweak often.

Remember…You Got This!

NUTRITIONAL FACTS
WORKS CITED

Batty, David. "Psychological Distress in Relation to Site Specific Cancer Mortality." *thebmj*. https://www.bmj.com/content/356/bmj.j108.

Becker, Joshua. "Stop Comparing Your Life. Start Living It." *Becoming Minimalist* (blog). https://www.becomingminimalist.com/stop-comparing-your-life-start-living-it/.

Britannica, T. Editors of Encyclopedia. "Circadian rhythm." *Encyclopedia Britannica*, November 19, 2019. https://www.britannica.com/science/circadian-rhythm.

Brown, Amy. "How Long Does It Take to Get Over a Divorce? 9 Things That Emotional Recovery Depends On." *ReGain*, July 30, 2021. https://www.regain.us/advice/divorce/how-long-does-it-take-to-get-over-a-divorce-9-things-that-emotional-recovery-depends-on/.

Brown, Brené. "The Power of Vulnerability." Filmed June 2010 in Houston, TX. TED video, https://www.ted.com/talks/brene_brown_the_power_of_vulnerability?language=en.

Coraci, Frank, dir. *Click*. 2006; Shreveport, LO: Columbia Pictures, 107 min.

Grimley, Bruce. "What is Neurolinguistic Programming, (NLP)?" *Universidad Central de Nicaragua.* https://www.achieving-lives.co.uk/files/Files/final%20dissertation%20v66%2012_12_2015%20for%20Viva%20on%2021_12_2015%20with%20corrections%20v66.pdf.

Heubeck, Elizabeth. "Boost Your Health with a Big Dose of Gratitude." *Florida Bar News.* https://www.floridabar.org/the-florida-bar-news/boost-your-health-with-a-big-dose-of-gratitude/.

International Self-Care Foundation, "A Brief History Of Self-Care." https://isfglobal.org/what-is-self-care/a-brief-history-of-self-care/.

James, Bev. "5 Ways To Avoid Making Fear Based Decisions." *the coaching academy.* https://www.the-coaching-academy.com/blog/2016/11/838.

Keyes, Ralph (2006). The quote Verifier: Who Said What, Where, and When. Macmillan. pp. 159–160. ISBN 0-312-34004-4.

Long, Jamie Dr. "Toxic Positivity: The Dark Side of positive Vibes." *The Psychology Group* (blog). https://thepsychologygroup.com/toxic-positivity/.

Lown, Beth A. "Compassion is a Necessity and an Individual and Collective Responsibility." *International Journal of Health Policy Management,* June 2, 2015. https://www.ncbi.nlm.nih.gov/pmc/articles/PMC4556578/#.

Mahesh, Maharishi. *"Science of Being and Art of Living: Transcendental Meditation."* Vlodrop, The Netherlands: Maharishi Vedic University Press, 2011.

Marshall, Garry, dir. *Runaway Bride*. 1999; Berlin, MD: Paramount Pictures, 116 min.

Merriam-Webster.com Dictionary, s.v. "addiction," accessed August 15, 2021, https://www.merriam-webster.com/dictionary/addiction.

Merriam-Webster.com Dictionary, s.v. "authentic," accessed August 13, 2021, http://www.merriam-webster.com/dictionary/authentic.

Elena, Peters. "How to Have Healthy Personal Boundaries." *makingMIDLIFEmatter*. https://makingmidlifematter.com/healthy-personal-boundaries/.

Peterson, Christopher, PhD. "Via Survey of Character Strengths." *Positive Psychology Center*. https://www.floridabar.org/the-florida-bar-news/boost-your-health-with-a-big-dose-of-gratitude/.

Physical Activity Guidelines Advisory Committee. "Physical Activity Guidelines for Americans; 2nd Edition." *U.S. Department of Health and Human Services*. https://health.gov/sites/default/files/2019-09/Physical_Activity_Guidelines_2nd_edition.pdf.

Purpose Focus Commitment. "Story about happiness: The meaning of the black dot on a white paper." https://

purposefocuscommitment.com/story-about-happiness-meaning-black-dot-white-paper/.

Research and Markets. 2021. "The Market for Self-Improvement Products & Services 2003-2025". *Marketdata LLC*. https://www.researchandmarkets.com/reports/5393508/the-us-market-for-self-improvement-products-and.

Rice, Jasmine. "The Art of Being Strong and Soft." *Good Things Are Gonna Come (blog)*. https://goodthingsaregonnacome.com/the-art-of-being-strong-and-soft/

Rice, Jasmine. "28 Day Gratitude Challenge." *Good Things Are Gonna Come* (online workbook). https://goodthingsaregonnacome.com/gratitude-workbook/.

Robins, Tony. "5 Strategies for Positive Thinking." https://www.tonyrobbins.com/positive-thinking/?AID=12703194&PID=100357191&cjevent=2b50238d11ad11ec81d57f-f80a1c0e0b&cjdata=MXxOfDB8WXww.

Ralston, Aron. "127 Hours: Between a Rock and a Hard Place." New York: Altria Books, 2005.

Schlessinger, Laura. "The 4 R's of Forgiveness." *DrLaura.com* (blog). https://www.drlaura.com/blog-the-4rs-of-forgiveness.

Shepherd, Janine. "A Broken Body Isn't a Broken Person." Filmed October 2012 in Kansas City, MO. TED video, https://www.ted.com/talks/janine_shepherd_a_broken_body_isn_t_a_broken_person?language=en.

Shirley, Matt. *Getting Over It Timeline* (Commissioned by Jasmine Rice: Reproduced by permission from Matt Shirley, 2020).

The Beatles. "Hey Jude." *Revolution*. Apple, 1968. LP.

Wolfinger, Nicholas. "Want to Avoid Divorce?" *Institute for Family Studies.* https://ifstudies.org/blog/want-to-avoid-divorce-wait-to-get-married-but-not-too-long/.

Womack, Kenneth (2014). The Beatles Encyclopedia: Everything Fab Four. Santa Barbara, CA: ABC-CLIO. ISBN 978-0-313-39171-2.

www.ingramcontent.com/pod-product-compliance
Lightning Source LLC
Chambersburg PA
CBHW022015290426
44109CB00015B/1173